OYSTER PERPETUAL SKY-DWELLER

ROLEX

danish design by · made by

LINDBERG

KINFOLK

ARCHITECTURE
Inside the buildings that move us, and the minds of their makers

RYUICHI SAKAMOTO
The composer inspired by his ow...

INTERVIEWS
Fabienne Verdier, Asif Khan and Sharon Van Etten

FEATURES
On suburbia, spoilers and the search for utopia

VOLUME THIRTY-ONE

KINFOLK

SPRING 2019

KINFOLK

The Weekend Edition — These are 48 hours ...
like. It's a judgment-free zone to be as still, ac...
as you please. Maybe you'll be the center of y...
enjoy a dinner for one, phone switched be...
Alternatively, your two days might entail a s...
rendezvous and soirees with good pals. No m...
the hours, make sure they're filled on your t...

12 Notecards and Envelopes

Premium
Subscription

Become a Premium Subscriber for $75 per year, and you'll receive four print issues of the magazine and full access to our online archives, plus a set of *Kinfolk* notecards and a wide range of special offers.

KINFOLK

FOUNDER & CREATIVE DIRECTOR
Nathan Williams

EDITOR-IN-CHIEF
John Clifford Burns

EDITOR
Harriet Fitch Little

ART DIRECTOR
Christian Møller Andersen

DESIGN DIRECTOR
Alex Hunting

BRAND DIRECTOR
Amy Woodroffe

COPY EDITOR
Rachel Holzma

COMMUNICATIONS DIRECTOR
Jessica Gray

PRODUCER
Cecilie Jegsen

PROJECT MANAGER
Garett Nelson

CASTING DIRECTOR
Sarah Bunter

SALES & DISTRIBUTION DIRECTOR
Edward Mannering

BUSINESS OPERATIONS MANAGER
Kasper Schademan

STUDIO MANAGER
Susanne Buch Petersen

PRODUCER (TOKYO)
Kevin Pfaff

EDITORIAL ASSISTANTS
Sylva Bocşa
Gabriele Dellisanti

CONTRIBUTING EDITORS
Michael Anastassiades
Jonas Bjerre-Poulsen
Andrea Codrington Lippke
Ilse Crawford
Margot Henderson
Leonard Koren
Hans Ulrich Obrist
Amy Sall
Matt Willey

WORDS
Zaineb Al Hassani
Alex Anderson
Rima Sabina Aouf
Elise Bell
Ellie Violet Bramley
John Clifford Burns
Katie Calautti
Stephanie D'Arc Taylor
Gabriele Dellisanti
Harriet Fitch Little
Moeko Fujii
Anindita Ghose
Bella Gladman
Tim Hornyak
Selena Hoy
Nick Narigon
Naomi Pollock
Debika Ray
Asher Ross
Laura Rysman
Charles Shafaieh
Ben Shattuck

CROSSWORD
Anna Gundlach

PUBLICATION DESIGN
Alex Hunting Studio

PHOTOGRAPHY
Gustav Almestål
Karel Balcar
Luc Braquet
Yuji Fukuhara
B.D. Graft
Aiala Hernando
Leonardo Holanda
Cecilie Jegsen
Romain Laprade
Flora Maclean
Christian Møller Andersen
Léa Nielsen
Michio Noguchi
Julien Oppenheim
Danilo Scarpati
Søren Solkær
Tezontle
Aaron Tilley
Zoltan Tombor
Alexander Wolfe
Yuna Yagi

STYLING, HAIR & MAKEUP
Line Bille
Taan Doan
Áron Filkey
Andreas Frienholt
Tara Garnell
Daisuke Hara
Candy Hagedorn
Cyril Laine
Kenneth Pihl Nissen
Stine Rasmussen
Tania Rat-Patron
Shimonagata Ryoki
Camille-Joséphine Teisseire
Pierre Yovanovitch

COVER PHOTOGRAPH
Romain Laprade

ISSUE 32
Kinfolk (ISSN 2596-6154) is published quarterly by Ouur ApS, Amagertorv 14, 1, 1160 Copenhagen, Denmark. Printed by Taylor Bloxham Limited in Leicester, United Kingdom. Color reproduction by PH Media in Roche, United Kingdom. All rights reserved. No part of this publication may be reproduced, distributed or transmitted in any form or by any means, including photocopying or other electronic or mechanical methods, without prior written permission of the editor-in-chief, except in the case of brief quotations embodied in critical reviews and certain other noncommercial uses permitted by copyright law. The US annual subscription price is $87 USD. Airfreight and mailing in the USA by Worldnet Shipping Inc., 156-15, 146th Avenue, 2nd Floor, Jamaica, NY 11434, USA. Application to mail at periodicals postage prices is pending at Jamaica NY 11431. US Postmaster: send address changes to Kinfolk, Worldnet Shipping Inc., 156-15, 146th Avenue, 2nd Floor, Jamaica, NY 11434, USA. Subscription records are maintained at Ouur ApS, Amagertorv 14, 1, 1160 Copenhagen, Denmark.

www.kinfolk.com

Published by Ouur Media
Amagertorv 14, Level 1
1160 Copenhagen, Denmark

The views expressed in *Kinfolk* magazine are those of the respective contributors and are not necessarily shared by the company or its staff.

SUBSCRIBE
Kinfolk is published four times a year. To subscribe, visit kinfolk.com/subscribe or email us at *info@kinfolk.com*

CONTACT US
If you have questions or comments, please write to us at *info@kinfolk.com*. For advertising inquiries, get in touch at *advertising@kinfolk.com*

HOUSE OF FINN JUHL

THE CHIEFTAIN TURNS 70

FEW THINGS NEVER CHANGE

WE CELEBRATE THE ULTIMATE CHAIR.

THE WAY IT IS. THE WAY FINN JUHL INTENDED IT.

NO GLITTERING ANNIVERSARY EDITION.

WHY CHANGE AN ORIGINAL?

finnjuhl.com

håndværk

A specialist label creating *luxury basics*.
Ethically crafted with an unwavering
commitment to *exceptional quality*.

handvaerk.com

Issue 32

Welcome

Kinfolk was founded in Oregon, operates out of Copenhagen, and has long had roots in Japan. In fact, since 2013, the magazine—and its ongoing exploration of quality of life—has been translated into Japanese at our sister office in the heart of Shibuya, Tokyo. On our most recent visit in March, local editors Mako Ayabe and Kota Engaku reminded us what life in the Japanese capital is like for those living there with a sense of intention and energy: one of navigable neighborhoods, courteous codes and cutting-edge culture. This is in stark contrast to the vision of Tokyo as a city that can feel impenetrable to the outsider.

For our 18-page guide, our photographer Romain Laprade and local writer Selena Hoy took recommendations from our Japan team and visited a dozen locations that, between them, paint a full picture of this varied metropolis: from a new rice specialist revitalizing a shuttered shopping district, to a store inside a house in upmarket, residential Shirokane. For our archive and feature profiles, we've chosen two women who made Tokyo their home a hundred years apart: Toko Shinoda, the 106-year-old abstract artist who still lives in the city center, and Yoon Ahn, the Korean designer who moved to the city in the early aughts, riding the peak of the city's street-style wave. When trying to decide what should feature in our Tokyo Issue, we thought a lot about how the city is represented in the popular imagination. In our latest longform essay, Moeko Fujii addresses this question head-on: Why, she asks, is Tokyo so often the canvas for Western visions of disaster and dystopia?

Perhaps because Tokyo is the world's most populous metropolis, spending time in the city left us longing for space to stretch out and enjoy the summer. Our Issue Thirty-Two fashion shoot takes place on a boat off the coast of Marseille, and our feature profile of Coco O tells the story of how the singer found room to breathe again by moving back to Copenhagen after several years in Los Angeles. In interviews with the architects Kengo Kuma and Bijoy Jain, we discover a common reverence for creating buildings in conversation with the nature and light that surrounds them.

Elsewhere, our writers and photographers seek to understand the seasonal restlessness termed "zugunruhe," how best to pack a suitcase, and—with the *Kinfolk* office now in full summer holiday mode—we decide to spend a day in the studio with Socrate, the most fashionable cat in Paris.

JOHN CLIFFORD BURNS & HARRIET FITCH LITTLE

"I really wanted to see what it was like doing everything on my own."
COCO O – P.40

Photograph: Aiala Hernando

1949 – 2019
standing the hard test of time. ✎ string.se

string® shelving system. made in sweden

string®

new. outdoor. galvanized.

"It's perhaps on the level of individual structures that Tokyo is easiest to grasp."
TIM HORNYAK – P. 176

Photograph: Romain Laprade

YŌNOBI

Dorval collection by SCMP DESIGN OFFICE
Edited by Lambert & Fils

lambert&fils

1
Starters

RIMA SABINA AOUF

On Self-Mythology

Don't be a cyclops—broaden your perspective.

Myths are more than stories. Late last century, some psychologists used mythology as a lens into our psyches. Influenced by Carl Jung's theories of the collective unconscious, they believed that archetypal characters and motifs recurred in cultures all around the world, and were also present in the minds of people who had no memory of reading them.

In this framework, the man who grew from feuding with his siblings to butting heads with colleagues was drawing fuel from Ares, the Greek god of war; the woman who had a prosaic desk job but measured her life in foreign discoveries and romances was mimicking the adventurer Hermes. The analysts argued that understanding the archetypes people had subconsciously chosen to emulate could help make sense of their life choices.

The pantheon of mythology offers up tricksters, teachers, protectors and pleasure-seekers, united by just one common trait: They're all heroes. Few idolize the sidekick or the villain, and almost nobody casts themselves as either one. But it's not solipsism that leads us to place ourselves at the center of the tale. Acting out the role of hero in our own lives is a form of subconscious storytelling that we all do naturally: We reflect on our history and pull its scattered milestones into a path that explains how we got here. When

these cohere into a sense of identity, the road ahead of us is gently lit.

But just because we have to be the hero, it doesn't mean we have to be The Hero. In his 1949 book, *The Hero with a Thousand Faces*, scholar Joseph Campbell argued that nearly every hero, across time and place, is a version of the same "monomyth." Campbell distilled the "Hero's Journey" into three sentences that have been highly influential (in fact, George Lucas had them in mind while writing *Star Wars*):

"A hero ventures forth from the world of common day into a region of supernatural wonder. Fabulous forces are there encountered and a decisive victory is won. The hero comes back from this mysterious adventure with the power to bestow boons on his fellow man."

Superficially, this Hero presents a romantic and empowering ideal. But they are also alone and separate. Their specialness is inherent to them and not owed to circumstance. We assume, but have no way to actually judge, that the hero is on the side of good.

If this is the hero image our subconscious is dredging up, then maybe our conscious mind should interject. Apart from all else, if part of us thinks we're on this Hero's Journey, how can we not go into crisis when we get literally any other ending besides victory?

So go ahead and be the hero. But be one armed with context.

Acknowledge your privileges and recognize all the people who enrich your life. Prepare to play the servant occasionally. Be open to any diversions, all denouements. And look critically at your narrative from time to time.

"It's immensely valuable to think about the story you're telling yourself, about yourself," says Charlotte Fox Weber, head of psychotherapy at The School of Life in London. "When we can re-author our own experiences, including challenging and re-scripting certain fossilized stories we've been carrying around, something shifts in our perception. It can be utterly transformative to review and adjust our stories. I like taking people to the past if it can be purposeful. Going to the past and simply staying there, stuck, is no good, just as anticipating and dwelling in the yet-to-exist future avoids reality and tends to be full of fantasy or anxiety."

As for that push-pull between bolstering the self and serving the greater good, it might be a hurdle to embrace rather than obliterate. "I love the tension between the individual and groups, and the sense of purpose and efficacy that can come from the collective," says Weber. "Something can get lost in the emphasis on one person's brand rather than thinking about working together, connecting, and building, and playing on strengths."

In *The Alter Ego Effect*, published this year, Todd Herman argues that athletes succeed by fashioning a "heroic self" that they step into the moment they enter play.

ALEX ANDERSON

On Air Conditioning

Just chilling? Think again.

At the turn of the 20th century, engineers referred to early air cooling technology as "man-made weather," a splendidly optimistic phrase suggesting that science was about to master those most unconquerable of all natural forces—the elements. In the decades that followed, "air conditioning" became the preferred term—a more pragmatic description of filtering, cooling and optimizing the moisture of interior air.

This less impressive label hardly diminishes the huge impact AC has had on the planet. The technology has made much of the world comfortably habitable for billions of people and facilitated the explosion of new cities. As historian Hal Rothman explains in *Neon Metropolis*, "air-conditioning was the catalyst for habitability" in the American South. Every visitor

to Las Vegas knows that almost nothing happens in the desert city without conditioned air. Even in the intense summer heat, it makes entertainment in the Mojave feasible. People have long traveled south to Las Vegas, Phoenix, and Miami during the winter to escape the rigors of frigid weather in New York and Chicago, but when air conditioning units became widely available in the middle of the last century, huge numbers of people moved south for good. Between 1950 and 2000, the US population tilted suddenly southward. From a sleepy 28 percent of the population, the South's share rose to 40 percent in those years.

Similar shifts are happening globally. China now has twice as many AC units as the US; as migrants move to the cities these

offer the same comfortable interiors from Xi'an to Hangzhou. Similarly, in São Paulo, in Riyadh, and in Mumbai, AC has allowed people, as Rothman might say, "to impress the template of their society on any landscape."

But tightly sealed windows and a steady mechanical hum often obscure the best aspects of these landscapes: the drifting scents of mowed grass and jasmine, the happy trills of mockingbirds, the churring of nighttime insects, the fluid sounds of wind and rain. As we move between cooled living rooms and offices, "outside" seems almost too uncomfortable to consider. So, we accept the constant thermal relief AC offers along with summers behind glass, and look out at the trees moving gently in a hot breeze as they cast cool shade on the empty grass.

Photograph: Leonardo Holanda, Model: Pedro Aboud

Left Photography: Courtesy of Dyson, Mr Porter and Everyday Needs. Right Photograph: Christian Møller Andersen

AIR HEADS

by John Clifford Burns

More dystopian than the history of conditioned air is its creeping commodification. Fresh air now comes in a spray can and is available to buy online. It is sold by a Canadian company called Vitality Air, which calls its products "a lifestyle" and its bottling process "painstaking and lengthy." An eight liter can costs US$32 (excluding shipping) and lasts for 160 breaths (or around 10 minutes). Among the FAQs to the founders, such as, "My product is very light. Are you sure there is anything in it?" and, sadly, "What does it taste like?" is a more urgent question perhaps better pondered by the United Nations: "What kind of person typically buys air?" (Answer: Canned capitalism is apparently popular in polluted parts of China.) Here are some options for improving, rather than importing, the air you breathe. (Top: Pure Hot+Cool Purifier, Heater and Fan by Dyson. Center: Feu De Bois scented candle by Diptyque. Bottom: Japanese paper fan from Everyday Needs.)

Well Hung

A quick look behind the curtain.

In his essay *The Curtain*, Milan Kundera evokes the revelatory act of "pulling away the curtain" when describing how the novel shows us the truths of life in all its mundane detail. A more memorable—and literal—example of the idiom occurs in the film *The Wizard of Oz*, when Dorothy's dog, Toto, drags aside an emerald curtain to show that the wizard is just a man operating a machine. "Pay no attention to that man behind the curtain," the wizard yells, desperate to maintain the façade of authority.

While we should pay attention to what is uncovered, we should also focus on the curtain itself. More than other barriers, it can imbue what it hides with a sense of importance. From those which conceal priests in confessionals to their red velvet counterparts in theaters, curtains convey a sense of expectation, promise and even menace. Their ripples suggest a constant restlessness, though they may hang still. And even when motionless, the shadows created by their sensuous folds evoke mysterious potentiality. Although easily opened, they nevertheless imply that whatever may be on the other side is inaccessible and even a world away.

That curtains attract surrealists is thus unsurprising. "I've always wanted to paint curtains," Francis Bacon once said. "I love rooms that are hung all around with just curtains hung in even folds." An interior designer prior to becoming a painter, Bacon shrouded numerous figures behind thin veils that at once obscure and illuminate, trap and reveal. René Magritte understood this paradox. Often employing their dual function of exposing and creating illusion, he took draperies as a metaphor for life's mystery: "We are surrounded by curtains. We only perceive the world behind a curtain of semblance. At the same time, an object needs to be covered in order to be recognized at all."

Both Bacon and Magritte would likely have been enticed by the Red Room in David Lynch's *Twin Peaks*. In this uncanny space, named for the crimson curtains which serve as its walls, language and movement are made strange. The room takes to the extreme what artists, singers, priests and actors alike know: that the curtain, whether pulled open or yanked shut, can reveal not only magical new worlds but also the strangeness of reality itself.

ASHER ROSS

Word: Tsundoku

An excuse to buy the books you won't read.

Etymology: The Japanese word tsundoku (積ん読) merges the kanji for *tsunde oku*, "to let something pile up," and *doku*, "to read." The hybrid term was something of a rhymed pun when it first appeared in print in the late 19th century. It can be translated loosely as "to buy reading materials and let them pile up."

Meaning: Tsundoku carries no pejorative sense in Japanese. Rather it connotes a cheerful whimsy: wobbly towers of unread books, each containing an unknown world. Minimalism is often beautiful, and it's usually a good idea to push back against our acquisitive impulses. But libraries should be given a pass. A well-read person becomes increasingly aware of how little they truly know, and their bookshelf should be treated as anything but a trophy case. Let *Middlemarch* glare down unread, along with the uncreased spines of those three books Joan Didion recommended somewhere. Their time will come. As the Lebanese-American scholar Nassim Nicholas Taleb once wrote, "The library should contain as much of what you do not know as your financial means...allow you to put there."

Marie Kondo, who more than anyone encapsulates the current fad for relentless paring down, made books a particular target in her hit Netflix series *Tidying Up*. This caused a backlash among book lovers, who seized on her personal preference for keeping "about thirty volumes at any one time." Kondo presses her clients to discard all but the most beloved items in their library, leaving the greatest hits and nothing else. She frames the decision this way: "By having these books, will it be beneficial to your life going forward?" The problem is that it's impossible to know. Our future selves are a mystery, and our minds will have mysterious needs. We can't predict which books will grow wiser with time, and which will wither on the shelf. Which, for example, should we keep for when our child's heart is broken for the first time? Which to read through blurry eyes at 3 a.m., New Year's Day, 2032? Books that "spark joy"—a favorite Kondo phrase—when we are young may bore us in middle age, only to enthrall us again later on. It's impossible to be sure, so we trust to chance, and intuition.

Tsundoku is a pleasurable word because it implies the freedom of not knowing. It treats reading not as a task, but as a journey in a pathless wood. If we are lucky we will have many selves in this life, and will experience all emotions, not just joy, down to their deepest hue. For each of these there's an unread book, biding its time.

Essayist Nassim Nicholas Taleb refers to any collection of unread books as an "anti-library": "The more you know, the larger the rows of unread books," he writes in *The Black Swan*.

Cecilie Bahnsen

Meet the designer who pairs hyperfeminine
fashion with sneakers.

Photography: Christian Møller Andersen

Before Cecilie Bahnsen founded her eponymous line in 2015, she worked as a print designer for John Galliano. "But I missed the 3-D element," she explains, speaking from Paris in between a flurry of fashion week appointments. Bahnsen's own line certainly makes the most of design's 3-D potential, with voluminous puffballs and exaggerated peplums. Here, the Danish womenswear designer celebrates subverting femininity and finally being able to afford her own clothes.

HFL: *Your clothes are often described as "girly." How did you dress growing up?* **CB:** I was definitely more experimental than my little sister. There was this same thing you see in the collection now of combining masculine and feminine; so I'd wear a poufy dress with a pair of wellies.

HFL: *Do you wear your own designs most days now?* **CB:** Yes. It's funny, because for the first year and a half I couldn't afford to wear my own clothes. I wasn't necessarily the sample size, and as a designer who started as a complete independent I didn't have the money to make them for myself. It's quite amazing to be able to wear them now. But I still wear pretty much everything with trainers!

HFL: *For pop-ups, you often create interiors in which to display your clothes. Why?* **CB:** I think dresses are sculptures, and I like the way they work in a room without being worn. I think it's also to give people an experience of a brand—especially if you don't have your own store. Whether it's with a space or a show, the music, or the way the girls walk, we try to create the feeling of being in a particular universe.

HFL: *You don't really fit the minimalist mold that Scandinavian labels are best known for. What do you gain from being based in Copenhagen?* **CB:** I learned a lot from working at big fashion houses like Galliano. It was so different to the Danish approach; you would do a print, then an embroidery on top of the print, and then put it on the biggest dress you could find. That idea of how elaborate a dress can be is definitely something I've kept in my own design. But I think there's an effortlessness to things in Denmark, both in the work atmosphere and also the way we dress. What you put on needs to be comfortable: It might be a big sculptural dress but it's really soft and nice so you don't feel like you're wearing something too precious.

Although Bahnsen intends to remain a womenswear designer, she is excited by the rise in androgynous fashion for men and the increasingly playful "mixing of styles" in menswear.

On the beauty of broken statues.

ELISE BELL

Stone Broke

Classical statues in museums rarely
look how their makers intended them
to. As well as missing limbs and
protrusions, many were originally
painted in gaudy colors.

You know of her, even if you haven't seen her: The Venus de Milo, Aphrodite of Milos. She's sculpted from marble, and her name alone speaks of a divine beauty unparalleled by anything mortal. And yet this most famous Venus is broken beyond repair: Both her arms are missing.

As with many celebrated classical statues, our appreciation of the Venus de Milo is shaped by loss. The American writer Charles Fort explained, "To a child she is ugly. When a mind adjusts to thinking of her as a completeness, even though, by physiologic standards, incomplete, she is beautiful." For archaeologists and historians, these incomplete masterpieces are a puzzle to be solved: Reconstructions of the Venus de Milo suggest her arms were in motion, holding a spinner with a spool or even a spear. But for most people, there is no pressing need to imagine limbs onto the goddess. In fact, it is through the absence of body parts that these classical figures become beguilingly modern.

Consider the surrealists. The dismembered forms of antiquity rear their headless bodies within the artwork of dadaists such as Jean Arp, and Dalí added drawers to a plaster cast of the Venus de Milo in one of his most famous works—pushing her already strange form into absurdity. During decades of violence and world wars, the incomplete statues, once whole, felt eerily close to the bone. While we are now seduced by the mysterious imperfections of statues, previous generations judged things differently. Tucked within the labyrinthine Glyptotek Museum in Copenhagen, there's a cabinet of noses. Made from plaster, the assorted noses speak to bygone practices of art restoration. As Victorians plundered Europe and beyond for ancient art to bring back home, molds were made to hide the damage and restore the works to their former glory. But tastes evolved, and these substitutes fell out of favor. The prosthetic noses were removed from the faces they had been designed to complete, and were displayed in a cabinet for posterity.

The Glyptotek noses are part of an aesthetic debate that has yet to be won: Should we repair what can be fixed, or leave the broken artworks as they are? As we race toward an age where technology and science can leave no mystery unsolved, there is perhaps a greater beauty in the things that exist as they truly are—with all of their imperfections.

Artwork: *Eye, Nose and Cheek*, F.E. McWilliam, 1939

AFTER SUN

by Harriet Fitch Little

Here's a riddle: What do you call a picture you can never actually look at? "Afterimage" is the name given to the fleeting shapes you see after staring at a bright light source: If you look at an undipped pair of headlights at night, a white orb will linger afterward; stare directly at the sun and you'll experience the same effect only amplified—possibly with extremely damaging consequences. This phenomenon, which occurs due to adaptations in photoreceptors in the retina, so intrigued the Polish avant-garde artist Wladyslaw Strzeminski that he made a career out of trying to recreate the ephemeral shapes of the projections in his work. Before attempting your own Strzeminski painting at home, invest in some shades to block out the most harmful rays. (Top: Raw Tobago by Mykita + Maison Margiela. Center: Uma by Sun Buddies. Bottom: Santa Black by Retrosuperfuture.)

Smaller Talk

Tips for conversing with children.

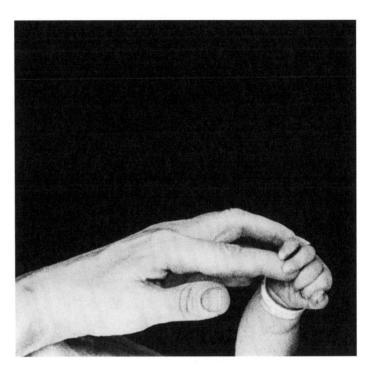

How do you talk to someone whose worldview appears different from your own? It's easy. When communicating with someone, say, on the opposite side of the planet, words tend to flow naturally. We know instinctively that understanding people involves gaining an insight into their life experiences.

By contrast, many of us struggle when speaking to children. The usual rules of human interaction seem not to apply and, instead, we fall back on mimicry and condescension. We try to connect by using exaggerated gasps of enthusiasm or forced emulation of their language and tone.

If you find your efforts to relate to children are often greeted with withering disdain, you might be surprised to hear that Sibéal Pounder, who writes humorous books for 7- to 9-year-olds, doesn't believe there's anything fundamentally different about children's internal logic. "I don't construct stories for children in a way that is different to how I would for adults," she says. When it comes to writing jokes, for example, the structures she uses are the same—it's just the content that's different.

This rings true when you think of popular children's stories and films. In everything from *Mary Poppins* to *Toy Story*, the plots are successful not because they are nonsense, but because the universes constructed within them follow the rationality of the adult world—and because the adults that create or exist within them take these seriously.

Abie Longstaff, another children's author, points out the mindfulness of a child's perspective. "I find children tend to be fixated on small details in stories. In my picture book, *The Fairytale Hairdresser and Rapunzel*, a bad witch goes to jail. At a literature festival, a small boy put up his hand and asked, 'When the witch is in jail who will look after her cat?'"

Where children do differ from us, Pounder suggests, is in the purity of their worldview. They're intrinsically optimistic, which is why small children believe they can outsmart criminal masterminds, rule worlds and slay dragons. "I wonder if it's an erosion over time of fundamentals such as optimism that make adults and children approach things slightly differently," she says. If that's the case, then the usual rules of conversation—questioning, debating and striving for empathy—seem as relevant to children as they do to adults. To crack the code, we just need to remind ourselves that, not so long ago, we also believed we were capable of anything.

In art, form is
as the thr
object
oc

A gra
to light, ta
the stone, and even
—by centuries of s
seashore. Much lighter th

ALL CUT UP

by Harriet Fitch Little

In 1942, British artist and army veteran Adrian Hill discovered the therapeutic benefits of drawing while recovering from tuberculosis in a sanatorium. As he later recalled in his book *Art Versus Illness*, the pencil drawings he made became "a form of escape which would combine the virtues of a creative and curative value." Art therapy, the phrase Hill coined, would go on to become a popular branch of mental health care. Today, therapists use clients' art as a projective technique—a way of getting them to express emotions that might otherwise go unspoken. As creative arts therapist Melissa Walker explained in a TED Talk on the subject: "There is an actual shutdown in the Broca's—or the speech-language area of the brain—after an individual experiences trauma." Drawing is a way to circumvent that blockage. But Hill, like most art therapists who followed him, had the advantage of being naturally good at art. How can the technique benefit people for whom the prospect of drawing stick figures and wonky sunsets feels insurmountably awkward? One alternative is collage therapy: pictures are assembled using pre-existing images, which become the jumping-off point for conversation. Even outside of a therapeutic setting, collage-making can relieve stress and encourage creative thinking. All you need is scissors, glue and a few magazines; you could start with this one. *Artwork: Form, B.D. Graft, 2015*

BEN SHATTUCK

Bird Brains

Unpacking our urge to fly away.

mer—a time to wander, to follow a path through the forest, to find a swimming hole and sun-warmed stones, to walk up a mountainside and fall asleep in the grass.

In songbirds, the urge to leave is signaled by a cocktail of hormones and environmental cues, mainly a steep decline of melatonin at night. In the spring, they fly to the northern hemisphere to raise their young on the bloom of insects wafting through the air. When winter starts to strip the land of food and the chicks have grown, everyone returns south, to the berries and seeds and bugs of South America, or Africa, or southern Asia. They've been doing this for millennia, inheriting the urge and ability to cover thousands of miles, over mountains and oceans, with a precision that still baffles scientists; an arctic tern will migrate the distance of the moon and back three times in her lifetime. It's an instinct so sharp and ancestral that some birds still end their migrations at the edge of where the ice caps once were, landing on the far side of a wall melted 15,000 years ago.

Zugunruhe in people doesn't always precede migration. You might just feel restless in the mind, a wandering imagination shaped by the changing seasons. "I ask to be melted," Henry David Thoreau journaled on an early April morning in 1852. He went on to explain his zugunruhe like this: "A few weeks ago, before the birds had come, there came to my mind in the night the twittering sound of birds in the early dawn of a spring morning, a semi-prophecy of it, and last night I attended mentally as if I heard the spray-like dreaming sound of the midsummer frog and realized how glorious and full of revelations it was. Expectation may amount to prophecy."

Summer was coming; he felt it in his dreams. Maybe Gustav Kramer's caged songbirds felt that too: their bodies not only shaking with anxiety to go blindly north, to follow the stars, but with the waking dreams of expectation, of the prophecy of early summer mornings beyond the horizon, of food and partnership, sex and parenthood, of perfect timing. When we want to take flight, perhaps it is just to escape the cold or our winter-bound homes—or maybe, as with Thoreau and the songbirds, it's a prophecy: We sense that something better is beyond the horizon, if only we take flight.

In the spring of 1949, in a coastal town in Lower Saxony, ornithologist Gustav Kramer trapped a few migratory songbirds in cages and put them outside. Every night, he noticed, the birds oriented themselves in the same direction, wings partially spread and quivering, their beaks tilted skyward. They hopped on their perches, agitated and excited, fluttering to the side of the cage facing their migration route. And because songbirds use the North Star to navigate, they did it only after sunset, when they could see the night sky.

Kramer called the condition *zugunruhe*, a German compound of *zug* (to move) and *unruhe* (unrest). Migratory restlessness.

It happens in people, too. There's a time to leave, when you feel a stirring. For most, it's in the fall, when, as Joni Mitchell sang in "Urge for Going," "The sun turns traitor cold / And all trees are shivering in a naked row." Others feel it in the spring; they are pulled outdoors when the land is unlocked from winter, when the ice and cold air roll away to leave a landscape filling with sum-

Photograph: *BLACK SUN #1*, Starling Murmuration by Søren Solkær (Denmark, 2016)

BEN SHATTUCK

How to Keep a Secret

What is out of sight is rarely out of mind.

What's so difficult about secrecy isn't hiding information from someone in a moment when they might discover it, but it's actually *living* with it—going about your day knowing there is something that you shouldn't say, turning it over in your mind when you're stuck in traffic or in bed waiting to sleep. The more you dwell on your secrets, researcher Michael Slepian discovered in his breakthrough 2017 study, *The Experience of Secrecy*, the more stress, anxiety and depression you feel. But, "Everyone has secrets," says Slepian. "Just because you have secrets doesn't mean you're a bad person. The average person has 13." The lonely mind, he advises, has only two releases: confession, or changing the way we think about secrecy.

BS: *What part of secret-keeping, exactly, is doing damage?* **MS:** Simply committing to the idea that you have information that cannot be known by some people leads to harmful effects. The only way we get around in this world is through our interactions with other people. We connect by sharing our experiences.

BS: *Do secrets affect their keepers differently?* **MS:** Secrecy hurts people who are prone to feel shame more than guilt. If you experience shame, you feel like you're a bad person, whereas guilt is more thinking, "I've done something bad." You can intuitively see why guilt is the more healthy and adaptive emotion: If you feel like you've done something bad, you can address that—you can make amends, apologize, not do it again. If you have shame, if you believe you're a bad person or worthless, the more your mind might wander into ruminating on your secrets. That's a lot more toxic and harmful.

BS: *So, if secrets are bad for us, why do we keep them?* **MS:** The question that often comes to people keeping their own secret is, "What damage would be done by revealing the secret?" The classic one is cheating on your partner and trying to decide whether to confess or not. Mostly people think, "You should obviously be truthful." But you have to consider whether the relationship can withstand that kind of confession. I'm certainly not advocating for infidelity by saying that, but you can imagine scenarios where revealing the secret can do a lot of damage. When that's the case, a person might think, "Well, maybe I just have to keep this secret." The question then becomes, "Who can I talk to about this? What can I do differently? How can I find a healthy way forward?" When you confide your secret to another person, you get a new perspective on it. Your mind ruminates on the secret less.

BS: *Does it matter who we offload our secrets to in order to feel better? Therapist or friend? In a confessional or with a partner?* **MS:** We haven't done the kind of research that looks at family member versus friend versus partner versus therapist versus confession booth, but we have looked at what personality traits you look for when confiding in someone. The more compassionate someone is, the more likely you'll confide in them. Whereas, the politer someone is—simply being nice, following social norms, social conventions—the less likely you are to confide in them. We also want to confide in people who are assertive, who can take charge, people who are going to go out of their way to help you figure out what to do next. Enthusiastic people, less so—the happy-go-lucky, bubbly, friendly person doesn't get confided in.

BS: *If we all have secrets—you say 13 on average—are we all doomed to have stress and anxiety in keeping them?* **MS:** When I think about this work, I see it as a cautionary tale with an optimistic note. The cautionary tale is that even when you don't have to hide your secrets, they still follow you, they're still with you and you're still alone with them. You don't have to hide them from anyone but they're still on your mind, and so they do quite a bit of harm. But the good news, the optimistic point is that finding new ways to think about the secret will improve your wellbeing. Confiding in another person will make a world of difference, as will focusing on the future: "What can I do going forward?" is a better way of thinking, instead of just brooding on the past, rehashing details of what happened. You can't change that.

Slepian's research found that secret-keeping had a pronounced effect on mindset: those weighed down by secrets overestimated the length and difficulty of tasks assigned.

Artwork: Abrazo Tezontle, 2017. Photograph: Courtesy of Tezontle / PEANA

GABRIELE DELLISANTI

Massimo Orsini

On the tiles with Mutina's CEO.

Photograph: Danilo Scarpati

Born into a family of ceramists in the northern Italian region of Emilia-Romagna, *Massimo Orsini* started handling clay as a child. In the early 2000s, he acquired Mutina—a once-traditional tile factory housed in a 1970s Angelo Mangiarotti-designed building on the outskirts of Modena. From making tiles consisting of thousands of hand-arranged mosaic pieces to designing 3-D terra-cotta bricks that double as room dividers, Mutina has quickly established a place for itself at the intersection of contemporary art and interior design. It's a passion that Orsini extends to his own life; he has a vast art collection, much of which he exhibits in a gallery-like setting at the new Mutina HQ. "When I look at art, I'm always looking for a specific aesthetic," Orsini explains. "I apply the same thought process at work when designing tiles, to understand how we can tell a story."

GD: *In 2005, you decided to purchase a struggling tile factory. How did you imagine its future?* **MO:** Mutina was born from the need to change perspectives on the world of ceramics. In Italy, their production has always been treated in a very classical way; often tile makers are using ceramics merely to copy other materials, such as marble or wood. I wanted to do things differently.

GD: *One of the things you're doing differently is bringing in designers from outside the world of ceramics to work on your collections. Why?* **MO:** I'm from Sassuolo, a small town in Emilia-Romagna, but I've been lucky enough to be able to travel and meet people who inspired me to question the certainties of the small community I come from. It's led me to develop a strong curiosity about all things contemporary, and a general attraction to the outlook of artists and designers. I wanted to have a dialogue with them, to learn more about their point of view, and eventually bring it all to the world of ceramics and tiles. The whole project started as a dialogue between artists about what contemporary design really means.

GD: *To date, you've worked with collaborators from seven countries, including the Spanish architect Patricia Urquiola and the Japanese designer Tokujin Yoshioka. Do different partnerships unfold in different ways?* **MO:** It's important for us to work with a group of people who can bring different perspectives. We didn't start Mutina just to sell tiles, but to create something interesting, beautiful and different. So far, we've collaborated with Japanese, German, French and Spanish designers. Working with such important designers is exciting because they're curious. The work that comes out of collaborations like that will stand the test of time.

GD: *What's the longest it's taken to design a new tile?* **MO:** Perhaps when we worked with Tokujin Yoshioka, who suggested the production of an extremely tiny mosaic. It required us to completely revolutionize our machinery.

GD: *As well as collaborating with artists in your day job at Mutina, you also collect art at home. Are you guided by the same interests in both spheres?* **MO:** I've always been inspired by minimalism in the visual arts. I like artists like Donald Judd and photographers like Luigi Ghirri, who comes from the same area as I do. In terms of the designers we work with, I admire those who spend loads of their time researching, such as Ronan and Erwan Bouroullec. Our collaboration with them took quite some time, but the end product is timeless and beautifully designed.

GD: *What made you decide to exhibit your personal art collection at the office?* **MO:** I like to keep my mind trained by researching artists from around the world, even if they're not connected to ceramics. Mutina for Art is a way of doing that. At the moment, we've got an exhibition called Surface Matters, and it showcases photographs from my own collection. We decided to do things a little differently—hanging the photos not on traditional white surfaces, but on walls clad with our own tiles. I'm very proud of it.

—

This feature was produced in partnership with Mutina.

"Tile production has always been treated in a very classical way. I wanted to do things differently."

Artwork: Borders by Karel Balcar. Courtesy of Reichenbach Collection, Repro Lhotak

DEBIKA RAY

How to be Charitable

Deciding which charities to support is a heavy responsibility. Who among us is really qualified to compare the moral worthiness of old people and children, trees and animals, cancer patients and diabetics? Should the question of who is deserving be based on our personal preferences and prejudices alone?

A movement called "effective altruism" is an increasingly popular solution to this quandary. We're all familiar with utilitarianism—Jeremy Bentham's notion that we should make decisions that result in the greatest good for the greatest number. Effective altruism, based on the ideas of philosopher Peter Singer, says we should apply a similar logic to philanthropy, allocating our money,

The case against kindness.

time and other resources in a way that will measurably do the most good. The UK-based Centre for Effective Altruism suggests we assess problems by their scale, the extent to which they are neglected and how solvable they are, then act accordingly—perhaps by choosing a career that has the mostpositive impact, or alternatively by finding one that pay you enough to be able to afford large donations.

In an age of data and algorithms it makes sense that such an approach to giving has struck a chord. "It's not an accident that a lot of people into effective altruism are from the hedge fund area, computer-based stuff, start-ups and the like," Singer said in an interview in 2015. It's hard to fault

the fundamental logic that resources could be allocated more effectively, and that evidence could play a part in that. Surely, most people's surplus income would be better spent on curing preventable illness than on personal frivolities. Can't we make complex comparisons between charitable causes and the impact of our assistance in an impartial way?

But such judgments are never objective; the measures we use to make them are themselves shaped by our values and preferences. Numbers alone cannot weigh poverty against environmental degradation, death against long-term suffering, human lives against those of animals. Few immediate benefits are apparent when undertaking the slow and incremental

hard work to overhaul deeply ingrained social ills or overturn injustice. Do older people deserve companionship only because it might extend their lives? And can women's empowerment be judged on wage increases alone? Human empathy—like the human experience itself—is always subjective.

Oxford professor Will MacAskill, an advocate for effective altruism, has suggested that saving a Picasso painting instead of a baby in a burning building may be the kindest course of action because one could then sell the painting and use the proceeds to save more children. Perhaps he is right, but wouldn't most of us sleep easier if we're left to assign our charitable funds to the causes that move us the most?

NAOMI POLLOCK

Kengo Kuma

Japan's modest blockbuster architect.

Kengo Kuma has a one-track mind. He designs architecture. He writes about architecture. He even thinks about architecture while soaking in the bath at his favorite hot spring. "There I can study the relationship between interior and exterior," says the designer earnestly. But these days Kuma doesn't have much time to kick back. His Hans Christian Andersen Museum is underway in Odense, Denmark, his V&A Dundee launched last year and his expansion of the Portland Japanese Garden finished in 2017. Not to mention the 2020 Olympic Stadium. Just blocks from his central Tokyo office, the arena is poised to open in November 2019. With projects popping up on multiple continents, Kuma is gently—but very definitely—making his mark around the globe.

NP: *What led you to become an architect?* **KK:** In 1964, when I was 10 years old, Tokyo hosted its first Olympic Games. At that time, my father, a businessman who was interested in design, took me to see Kenzo Tange's stadium. He had shown me other modernist buildings but this one was so symbolic and structurally unique. It shocked me. I still remember the way natural light came down from the ceiling and landed on the pool. It looked like heaven. On that day, I decided to become an architect.

NP: *Did the house you grew up in impact your decision as well?* **KK:** Yes. I grew up in a traditional style house in an area called Okurayama, which is between Tokyo and Yokohama. In the 1960s, Okurayama was just a train station and some shops. Pretty much everything else was rice paddies. We lived in a small wooden house built by my grandfather who was a doctor in Tokyo but liked to farm on the weekends. The house's *engawa* porch was my favorite space—I remember sitting there and waiting for my mother. In front of the engawa, I often made *takibi* fires and roasted sweet potatoes in the ash. Especially in the wintertime.

NP: *You weren't worried that you'd burn the house down?* **KK:** [Laughs] No!

NP: *Did you design the house that you live in now?* **KK:** No. The house was designed by my wife, Satoko, who is also an architect. If I designed it, she might not have been so satisfied. But we have now lived there for almost 20 years. I especially like the big roof terrace from which I can see all around my neighborhood.

NP: *You went to New York to study at Columbia University. In what way did that experience change your view of Japan?* **KK:** Before going to New York, I was not interested in Japan's traditional buildings and gardens. Being there made me question my identity and background. In my apartment, I had two tatami mats and a tea set so I could share the Japanese tea ceremony with my American friends. The mats were very expensive—I

Kuma's low-rise, lattice timber stadium for Tokyo's 2020 Summer Olympics was commissioned after an initial proposal for a futuristic Zaha Hadid design was scrapped for being unpopular and over-budget.

had to buy them from a Japanese carpenter in LA—but they helped me feel my "Japaneseness."

NP: *And while you were in New York, you wrote your first book?* **KK:** Yes. In 1985, I wrote *Jutaku Ron* which was a critique of Japanese architects. At that time, Tadao Ando was very influential in Japan. My friends and classmates were copying his designs. They were beautiful buildings, but not comfortable. And that was not what I wanted to create. Design can be very egotistical when architects only try to promote their own aesthetics. Many young designers thought that that should be their goal. But I tried to criticize that kind of aesthetic exclusivity and open architecture up to society. This was the beginning of my career. Now I'm writing a theoretical book titled *Ten, Sen, Men* meaning "point, line and surface." It was inspired by the famous book by Wassily Kandinsky, *Point and Line to Plane*, which was based on his lectures at the Bauhaus in the 1930s. I read that book in high school, just before studying architecture. It exposed me to

many ideas about composition.

NP: *How do you focus your mind on writing?* **KK:** My daily architectural practice pushes me toward writing because of the frustrations caused by differences of opinion with the client and other issues. Through writing, I can find meaning in those stresses. And then it becomes similar to psychotherapy. Sometimes writing shows me the deeper meaning of what I am designing which is kind of like a sport. As in tennis, when the ball comes, you just hit it without thinking deeply. But writing gives me the distance to see the meaning of each shot. Any one of them could be a turning point in my design.

NP: *What else do you do in your spare time?* **KK:** I like eating and drinking good wine, which also relates to design since architecture and food both involve communication between materials.

NP: *Do you like to cook?* **KK:** I myself am not a good cook. But I have many friends who are chefs and I learn a lot from them. Western food is more taste oriented but Japanese food is more

design oriented. It uses good ingredients and simple techniques; the cooking process is not so complicated. In many ways, it is about combination and proportion, which is very similar to what I do. The relationship of a column's size and material to the space as a whole is the same as the relationship between food and the dish that holds it. A good Japanese chef is a good designer.

NP: *Do you have a favorite food?* **KK:** I like simple food. Whenever I travel, I like to try local food and wine. That is the easiest way to research a place. Through the food, I try to find the essence of that place.

NP: *What foods capture the essence of Tokyo?* **KK:** Tokyo is… *tachi-kui soba*, the noodles eaten while standing in the station. It's cheap but delicious food. I like that experience very much.

NP: *Do you think that Japanese culture has a unique sensitivity or sensibility toward materials?* **KK:** I think so. Especially where size is concerned. In our design process, we talk about the size of the edge of every element. Those dimensions can change the user's experience totally. Japanese people understand this very well. We also consider the visual "noise," or texture, of materials. If one "noise" is too loud, it will cancel out the others. But if the "noises" are well-balanced, they can coexist. We Japanese cannot live with just one material—the assortment of different chairs in this conference room is a case in point. The traditional Japanese house is another example. The hidden rule of coexistence is smallness and lowness. In a tatami mat space, everything is low and small. It was the same in old Japanese cities where buildings of different design and scale worked together because everything was low. Smallness is also the basis for my new Olympic Stadium where the façade is covered by wood planks whose dimensions were inspired by the standard size of wood columns in Japanese houses. That dimension belongs to our daily life and is very nostalgic for us. In this 80,000-seat stadium, people will perceive the dimension of the small house.

"Before going to New York, I was not interested in Japan's traditional buildings."

2
Features

Meet the singer who left her band, record label and life in Los Angeles to move home to Copenhagen and go solo.

C O

Words by *Zaineb Al Hassani*, Photography by *Aiala Hernando* & Styling by *Kenneth Pihl Nissen*

"I got so frustrated at always being treated like a princess on a pea."

On a Tuesday afternoon in a dark, smoky bar in Copenhagen, regulars chat about everything and nothing. No one pays much attention to a young woman in the corner booth, playing with the sleeve of her fluffy sweater as she talks.

Coco O doesn't impose herself on a room. In fact, the Danish singer-songwriter comes off as a little shy. But her voice—and *what* a voice—is her talent. It's taken her on a journey from being on a major label and living in Los Angeles, to having no label and living back in Copenhagen, on the cusp of releasing a solo album.

A decade ago, Coco O teamed up with songwriter and producer Robin Hannibal to form Quadron, a soul-pop act. Their self-titled debut album would eventually lead to a move to LA and opportunities for Coco to work with American musicians and pick up a slew of big-name fans along the way. Sometimes, Coco says, it felt like living in a fairytale—but it wasn't all magical.

"I had a team of, I don't know how many people, and I got so frustrated sometimes at always being treated like a princess on a pea," she says, referring to the Hans Christian Andersen story. "People would say, 'Oh, you just do what you do, and we'll take care of the rest. I really wanted to see what it was like doing everything on my own.'"

But she was hard-pressed to figure out what "do what you do" was supposed to mean. In between Quadron's two albums (their 2009 debut was followed by *Avalanche* in 2013), Coco enjoyed a moment in the spotlight: She was featured on *The Great Gatsby* soundtrack and found herself bolstered by many influential supporters. Rapper Tyler, the Creator once said she had "the voice of an actual angel."

Now, at the age of 31, almost six years after her last Quadron record, and almost two years since she moved back to Copenhagen, Coco is figuring out how to go it alone. Part of that means looking back to where it all started, in the city where she grew up. With a musician for a father, Coco—who was born Cecilie Maja Hastrup Karshøj but has been called Coco since she was a kid—spent her childhood surrounded by music

Along with Kendrick Lamar, Quadron collaborated with Pharrell Williams when recording the album *Avalanche*, but ultimately cut the song from the final tracklist.

Hair: Line Bille, Makeup: Stine Rasmussen

FEATURES

paraphernalia. At eight or nine, she performed her first gig of sorts: On stage at her elementary school, Coco sang a verse from the Bill Withers song *Ain't No Sunshine*. She remembers the elation she felt when her voice carried over the room; singing was something that came easily to her.

As a teenager, Coco studied music for a year at an *efterskole*—a Danish residential school where pupils are given more freedom to pursue nonacademic subjects. Soon after, she started to take part in jazz sessions with local musicians. The urge to perform really began to take hold: She joined Boom Clap Bachelors, a Danish collective of musicians, producers and DJs that included her future Quadron partner, Robin Hannibal.

Then, in 2008, Boom Clap Bachelors stopped producing music and Quadron emerged from the ashes. Their debut album was heavily influenced by '70s soul music, a sound Coco says was not popular in Denmark at the time. "We were a little bit ahead of our time. Ahead or late," she laughs.

But people were paying attention. After using Myspace to market themselves, Quadron somehow landed on the radar of KCRW radio DJ Anthony Valadez, who broadcasts from the campus of Santa Monica College in California. It would be the beginning of their ascension to international airwaves. The album was played on heavy rotation across the US, and it wasn't long before they were approached by an indie label, Plug Research, and a manager. "[He was] like, 'Yo, I was crying to your music in the airport, I really want to work with you guys,'" Coco recalls, smiling. It was a turning point for the duo—who did not feel their music was getting the recognition it deserved back home—one that was solidified by their first US gig in Los Angeles. Playing to a sold-out audience and finding themselves surrounded by people wanting autographs was overwhelming, says Coco.

With a strong buzz behind them, the band moved to Epic Records in 2011, and also to LA. Coco got a good taste of the glamorous side of the music industry. There were the parties, including one thrown by Prince, and meetings with legendary music producers such as Jimmy Iovine. And there was the time that Coco was chosen by Jay Z to perform "Where The Wind Blows" for *The Great Gatsby* soundtrack. But it wasn't as glamorous as people think, she says. "It was really fun going to the premiere of *The Great Gatsby*. That was a big moment for me," she says. "But besides that… it sounds better than it feels."

A more meaningful collaboration, she adds, was that with rapper, songwriter and producer Kendrick Lamar, who invited Quadron to his studio after coming across Boom Clap Bachelors. Their sessions would lead to Lamar featuring on *Avalanche*. Released to much acclaim, it would also be Quadron's last album.

Given the way the band started, and how each member viewed its trajectory, their ending was perhaps inevitable, says Coco. "It wasn't my master plan when I started my career that I was like, 'Oh, I'm going to be in this band with Robin forever,'" she says over the phone later in the week, while she busies herself packing for a flight. "It was more like, 'Let's just see where it takes us.' I think we did pretty good."

Hannibal, says Coco, preferred being a producer over being in a band and dealing with things like interviews or photo shoots. He also didn't like performing live, meaning that on most tours Coco performed alone. At some point, she reflects, the balance between them started to shift and she became overwhelmed.

It was a feeling that had followed the musician for several years—both as a result of moving her life to LA and due to the responsibilities that came with being signed to a major label. Coco knew she would eventually go solo. It was just a matter of when. "Anything can happen, so if you don't know who you are without that other person, you're going to be fucked at some point," she says. "You have to figure out who you are on your own."

After the split, Hannibal went on to found the band Rhye and Coco was offered a solo deal. But it wasn't the right time, or the right place. Though the band was meant to end, she says, the decisions she made following its demise might not be the same decisions she would make today. Perhaps a bit stubborn, and maybe a little unrealistic, Coco decided to fire "everyone and everything" in order to start afresh. "Not everyone can make that dancefloor track, and I think, why should I compete

"We were a little bit ahead of our time. Ahead or late…"

"She sings with attitude, but not aggression. Even when she's angry, she comes off as sweet," is how *The New York Times* once described Coco's voice.

In 2013, Coco featured alongside Erykah Badu on the Tyler, The Creator track "Treehome95."

"I don't even like the music on the radio most of the time, so why try to compete with something I don't even enjoy?"

with that when every single person in the studio right now is trying to make a number one hit?" she says. "I don't even like the music on the radio most of the time, so why try to compete with something I don't even enjoy? It would be weird."

As she worked on her new master plan, life changed somewhat for Coco. She stayed in LA and continued to make music. But soon, she realized, she was trying to replicate the sound and partnership she had created with Quadron. It was also a struggle to live in a city where apartments were hard to come by, and expensive.

And then, home called. A friend was renting his apartment in Copenhagen for a good price. "It was springtime, I was like, 'Fuck it, I need to go to Denmark, save my money, see what it feels like to be back,'" she says.

It was the right choice. "I felt so relieved. To escape back to this little pearl of a nation. To Christianshavn, which is so idyllic. I had this amazing summer, then I met the love of my life; everything was just going well." Throughout all this—from Quadron ending to her moving home—Coco continued to write music. And when that new relationship ended, she turned her heartache into a two-track EP, *Dolceaqua*, which she released last year.

"Tragedy comes in many forms," Coco wrote in a Facebook post accompanying the May release. "This winter, mine was in [the] shape of a middle-aged man. I guess sometimes things [have] to turn really, really bad in order to become good. His gift to me was inspiring me to write these songs." While the pain is palpable on the EP, especially so in "Bled for You," the effect her music has both on her and the people

that listen to it gives everything a sense of purpose. As she continues to pack, she talks on the phone about her gig the night before and how she performed entirely new material. It was like a "photo album" of that relationship, she says, "going back in time and remembering how it felt—both the feelings I had for the guy but also the aftermath."

Two other singles followed *Dolceaqua* at the end of last year, "1000 Times" and "Know It." Though the songs are slightly more upbeat than the EP, a clear style is emerging. Coco's voice is haunting but simple, making it easy to liken it to Sade's. It's a comparison she'll happily accept: "She is one of my favorites. She has a very soft voice, it's very emotional," Coco says. The singers also share a lack of technical training but a remarkable sense for tone.

Coco is determined to produce an album this year. It is a promise she has made to herself, and one that seems ever closer to being realized after her concert. But it's a big step for the musician, who struggles sometimes with the creative process. "I can go back and forth so many times that I actually now wake up, six years later, and I'm like: 'What! Why didn't I just put out that first album that I kind of already made?!'"

Now, with a clear target in sight, would Coco say her desires have changed over the years? Though she still aspires to "big things, grand things," the other side of the industry—the business side, and the cynical way pop music is created—has shaped her long-term plans, she says.

"When I was little I wanted to be as big as possible," Coco explains, pausing to laugh. "Now, I want to be as big as possible within the realistic measurements of the music I want to create."

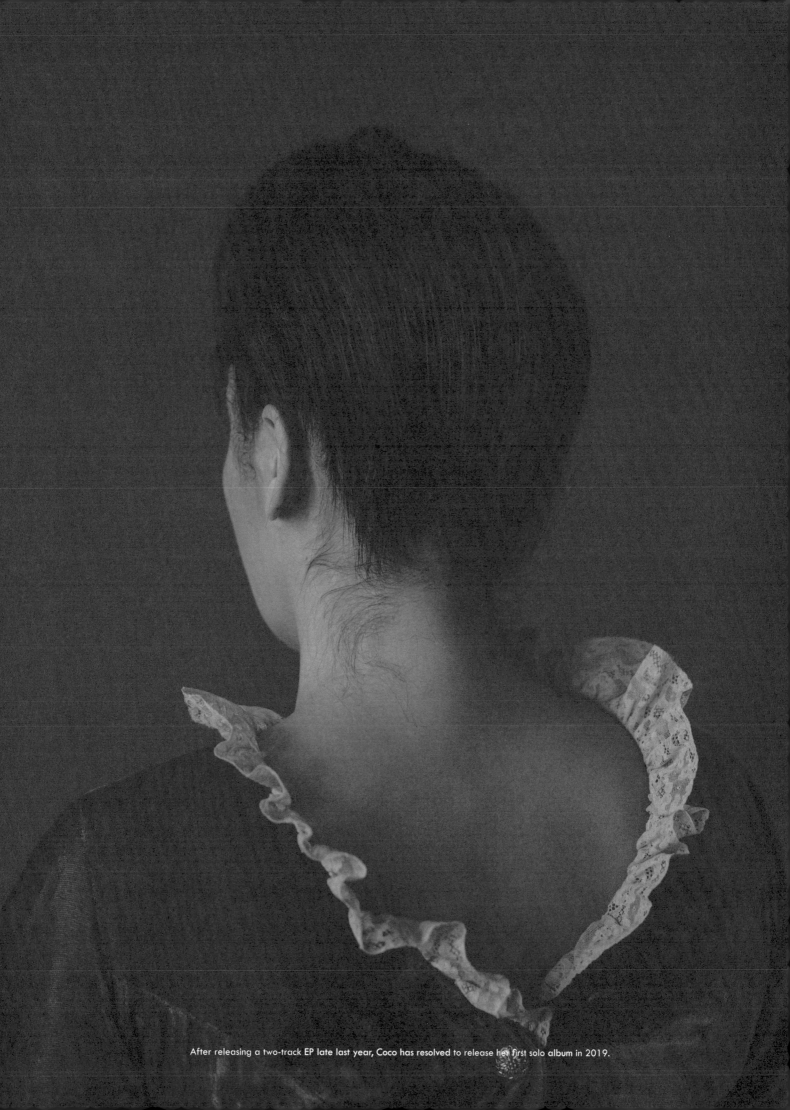

After releasing a two-track EP late last year, Coco has resolved to release her first solo album in 2019.

At Work With:
Bijoy Jain

The philosophically-inclined architect behind Studio Mumbai speaks to *Anindita Ghose* about exporting his vernacular (and award-winning) style. Photography by *Alexander Wolfe*

"A building is immobile, but that doesn't mean it doesn't have the capacity to move."

It's a working Sunday for Bijoy Jain, the architect and founder of Studio Mumbai, when we meet in the compound that houses both his studio and home in central Mumbai. Once a tobacco warehouse, the premises—like much of the surrounding neighborhood—bears vestiges of the city's industrial past; the rusty sheet-metal entrance gate offers no indication of the abundant foliage and light within.

Jain's studio is known domestically for a number of lauded projects, largely residential, that emphasize natural materials and vernacular construction.

Increasingly, the architect's respect for light, air and water is in demand with clients around the world following on from a series of successful showcases at biennales and exhibitions in cities including Venice, London and Melbourne. Before he has to leave for the south of France, where he will work on a new commission for a vineyard, he takes the time to sit (alongside his puppy Chucho) in his studio's sunlit courtyard to talk about the impact of the '60s, the evolution of his practice and swimming.

AG: *You've said that architecture is a physical and material manifestation of what it means to be human.*

What can we understand about humanity from the buildings we see around us today? BJ: The human body breathes, but most of what we're seeing around us now are non-breathing containers. In years gone by, we came from spaces that would breathe. For me, the idea is to reclaim that. A building is immobile, but that doesn't mean it doesn't have the capacity to move. It's how you use materials: It's the way that light moves, the way that water enters, that gives it movement.

AG: *Your portfolio was intensely regional and specific until recently. How are you transporting your philosophy now that you're building abroad?* BJ: When you travel abroad in winter, do you dress as you dress here? What you're doing in that gesture is enabling yourself to negotiate the landscape. We are attuned to understanding climate. It's a fundamental phenomenon... It's got nothing to do with whether I live in India or Europe or Timbuk-three!

AG: *You don't feel pressure to continue a certain aesthetic?* BJ: I would be holding prejudice if I did.

AG: *Still, there must be a common thread that runs through all of Studio Mumbai's projects?* BJ: The first work I did in architecture school took me back to a water tank I used to play in as a kid. Water has always been at the center of my work in some way or the other since then, be it present or absent. That's where growth can occur. Where there is water, there is air, there is light. The color of the sky is based on the reflection of water. That's our topology. For me, it's a universal connection. I don't know if it has to do with the fact that I used to be a swimmer.

AG: *You swam for India. You've swum across the English Channel! Does that experience inform your self-discipline at work?* **BJ:** Both are equally demanding. I'm fortunate to have had that experience as it has allowed me in certain ways to be in this profession. It demands the same kind of examination at the practice every day.

AG: *Much of your work is about storytelling, like the Ganga Maki Textile Studio that you built in the foothills of the Himalayas for the textile designer Chiaki Maki. I read that she asked for the building to be made in the same way as her indigo-dyed textiles.* **BJ:** We're also working on a winery in the south of France and we have committed to the client that the project will emerge in the same way that they make their wine—centered on the idea of terroir. Wine—for its full potential to be realized—requires time. The building will have the same quality. It will evolve and improve over time. I'm drawn to the phenomenology of that kind of engagement, in which the building mimics the subject.

It's also interesting to see if the physical mass of a building can have its own mechanism independent of man. If, for whatever reason, there was a war that wiped us out, would these structures offer something that can allow the reconstruction of life? A formal water source, perhaps. In Mumbai, entire neighborhoods have been constructed because of a water source.

AG: *Before you delivered the Geoffrey Bawa Memorial Lecture in 2012, you spoke about the time you met Bawa, the acclaimed Sri Lankan architect. How much does your inside-outside approach to building owe to what he said to you, that "There is too much architecture between me and the view."* **BJ:** It was a very poignant moment: to reflect back on the idea of what it means to build. I had just graduated and was visiting Sri Lanka with friends, but I knew I was going to meet him. I think what he was referring to is the idea of the moment of the

Jain's repertoire also includes art. Using natural materials similar to those in his architectural practice — cow dung, lime plaster, basalt, ash, clay, and banana fiber — he presented his second solo exhibition in December 2018 at Chemould Prescott Road gallery in Mumbai.

FEATURES

Over the last 16 years, Studio Mumbai has collaborated with British artist Muirne Kate Dineen to create the colors featured in its projects using only natural pigments.

"Modernity, in my view, is misrepresented."

threshold. Where is the threshold? **AG:** *Is it where home ends and the world begins?* **BJ:** Or where you remain suspended with the idea of man in nature. And nature in man. There's that point of equilibrium and I think that's what he was referring to. Looking for that space, which is a free space.

AG: *You call yourself a '60s child —blue jeans and Jim Morrison. Interestingly, it was also a very pertinent decade for modernist architecture.* **BJ:** I was born in the '60s. There was a revolution taking place. We had just come out of a war. Cultural shifts were happening. Everything was colliding and merging. In India, we had Archie comics and the Amar Chitra Katha comic book series. You were reading both at the same time as you were listening to Indian classical music and Deep Purple. Modernism was thriving. People came in from other parts of the world. Le Corbusier finished work on Chandigarh. Louis Kahn built the National Parliament of Bangladesh. Colonization was slowly breaking down worldwide. It was an opportunity. I don't want to call it a clash.

AG: *And are you comfortable with the perception that your work bridges the gap between contemporary modernism and the vernacular?* **BJ:** No interest in that at all. Modernity, in my view, is misrepresented. This idea of what does it mean to remain contemporary? The way I look at it is to be outside of dogma. So, to say modernism marries vernacular is misplaced. Both had the same aim—to begin with anyway.

AG: *You teach in the Swiss Academy of Architecture in Mendrisio. What would you advise students wishing to build their own sustainable practice?* **BJ:** The best starting point is to reflect on how you want to participate. How you want to inhabit the landscape. What can you do to enable the equation with the landscape to be one that is nourishing as opposed to one that is depleting? We already have had many people before us who've left so much for us to observe. Be it Ajanta and Ellora in India, be it Petra, the Egyptians or Japan. We've got all of that to reflect on. That's our lineage.

AG: *What is your dream project?* **BJ:** I'd love to do a school, a shelter for animals and a place where the elderly can heal. Yes, maybe all in one space. Gandhi had said the quality of a nation is in how the flora and fauna are cared for. And also the old.

STUDIO MUMBAI IN JAPAN

by John Clifford Burns

Jain recently undertook his first permanent project outside of India. Opened late last year in the Japanese port city of Onomichi, LOG (Lantern Onomichi Garden) is a 1960s apartment block that Studio Mumbai was commissioned to renovate into a hotel and community space. Here, Jain has employed his signature handcrafted interiors and application of natural materials, such as the abundant use of washi paper in each of the six guest bedrooms. Elsewhere, in spaces such as the café, gallery and shop (which stocks some of Jain's furniture designs), the city's residents can gather together for workshops focused on local history and culture.

Jain's respect for the land on which he's building sometimes extends to him using no mechanical tools on a project.

Summer

A boat in France. A quiet bay. We'll sail until *the wind changes.*

At Sea

Photography by Luc Braquet & Styling by Camille-Joséphine Teisseire

Above: Stephanie wears a swimsuit by Morgan Lane and a swimming cap by Eres. Right: Julien wears trousers by Hermès.
Stephanie wears a swimsuit by Hermès and a Maison Michel headband.

Julien wears swimming trunks by Pullin. Overleaf: Julien wears a T-shirt and shorts by Hermès.

Left: Julien wears a Breton top from Petit Bateau, and shorts and a belt by Ralph Lauren. Above: Stephanie wears trousers by Sportmax, a blouse by Rochas and a hat by Laurence Bossion.

Below: Stephanie wears a dress by Sandro and a belt by Sportmax. Right: Julien wears a shirt by Ralph Lauren, shorts by Hermès and uses Hermès binoculars.

Above: Julien uses a towel by Hermès. Right: Stephanie wears a dress by Rochas and a scarf and leather sandals by Hermès.

Home Tour:
Todoroki House

In Tokyo, *Alex Anderson* discovers a house of two
halves, designed to preserve the dual tradition of
sociable openness and familial privacy in the heart
of the city. Photography by *Yuna Yagi*

Tane's projects always emphasize what he terms the "memory of place." He is insistent that a building project cannot be relocated once a site has been decided on.

Humid air rises up from a deep ravine in Tokyo's Todoroki Park. Ferns spread in the shade, catching bright shafts of sunlight. Water trickles in the stillness and, high above, tree leaves rustle dryly in a hot summer wind. Architect Tsuyoshi Tane describes such a moment as the impetus for an unusual idea he had for a new house—two houses really, one for dry conditions on top of another for wet conditions—that would soon become Todoroki House, completed last year.

In his Paris atelier, Tane and his team searched for house styles to match his vision. "We were intrigued and surprised to find so many different houses for wet and dry climates," he recalls. Their earliest concepts involved the simplest of operations: collaging a photograph of a hot-dry-climate house onto one of a hot-wet-climate house. Over dozens of iterations, incongruous juxtapositions began to seem congenial. Tai-chi Saito, the client for the house and its landscape designer, explains that there was an "aura of inevitability" to the project, which followed naturally from thinking about it in terms of archaeology. First, Tane considered primitive architectural responses to climate, and then he observed the natural order of the compact site, with its low, shaded north side and dryer, more exposed southern aspect.

A process of archaeological research guides all of Tane's projects; he unearths deeply embedded memories in each site he works with to inform its new direction. This approach powerfully shaped a competition proposal for the Estonian National Museum, a commission he and his partners at Dorell Ghotmeh Tane won in 2005. In the museum, which opened in 2016 to global acclaim, overcoming unhappy memories from the Soviet occupation seems to construct a new trajectory for Estonia. Tane's intellectual process also orients two major exhibitions of his work that opened in Tokyo late last year. One of these, *Archaeology of the Future—Digging & Building*, exemplifies the atelier's attitude. Hundreds of images and models mounted on fragments of reclaimed building material demonstrate work inspired by the past.

But Tane is not trying to recreate the past; he combines his archaeological inquiry with a dedication to designing for the reality of today. This proved to be especially challenging at the Todoroki site. Tane recalls that the tight urban context and strict Tokyo codes initially seemed unfriendly to their efforts, pushing the design toward an unsatisfyingly

"What if there were no modernization? How would houses be in Japan?"

conventional house form. This amplified a realization he had while designing another house in Japan several years ago: In their increasingly standardized houses, people were "missing connections to the earth" and losing a sense of the crucial balance between Japanese *ima* and *nema* spaces—between the almost public living room and more private sleeping areas. "What if there were no modernization?" Tane mused. "How would houses be in Japan?" In its scale, Tokyo (where Tane was born) intensified these concerns: how could a new house offer an abiding sense of Japanese life, of familial openness and quiet privacy in the city?

The Todoroki House gradually took shape in two slightly irregular, eight-sided parts. The lower, earthbound living space expands toward a north garden. The sleeping spaces rise above it into the foliage of the surrounding trees—borrowed from the neighbors, Saito explains, in the tradition of *shakkei* (incorporating background landscape). A wooden door opens into the house from the small south-facing entry court. A low stone stoop holding potted plants reaches out from the door, stopping short in the gravel yard. Parts of the upper stories cantilever discreetly over the entry and its roughcast wall, throwing them into shadow. Plants from a garden terrace above trail down, wavering quietly in the breeze. A rough pile of boulders tumbles downward from the door toward the lush shade of the north garden. Saito explains that in designing the court and garden for the house, he "wanted to express dynamic *wabi-sabi*," a fleeting, imperfect beauty.

The fine subtlety of this composition is easy to miss. The cedar cladding over the door, for example, tightly follows the irregular angles of the cantilevered bays, each corner slightly different. The woodworking is exquisite, but its many variations are hardly noticeable. Tane compares the skill of the carpenter to that of a sushi master. The roughcast walls of the lower house exhibit a different kind of craft. Formed partly with soil excavated for the foundations, their color and texture complement the stones and gravel of the court. Inside, the vestibule beyond the entry is a low, dark mezzanine that overlooks the living space and expansive windows toward ferns, palmettos and bird-of-paradise plants in the moist shade beyond. Saito selected more than 60 plant varieties from around the world for the garden, to ensure perpetually green foliage and "flowers and fruits in all four seasons." Despite the close prox-

imity to neighbors and huge panes of glass, there's a serene sense of privacy. Stairs descend into the sun-dappled living area, where reading, conversing, cooking and dining spaces are woven together. Robust mid-century wooden furniture accentuates the earthy warmth of the space. Partially below ground level, the room's low horizon extends to the roots and trunks of plants in the garden. The roughcast walls turn in from the exterior to form a deep space for the dining table, and beyond it, a small sheltered study. Tane explains that these heavy, earthbound walls add to the comfort of the interior, absorbing moisture and retaining heat. In the summer, they help keep the space cool as warm breezes whisper through open windows. In the winter, warmth drifts up from the walls and heated stone floor to the private areas of the house above.

The open stairway climbs toward the surprisingly bright spaces of the sleeping rooms upstairs. It lands on the parquet floor of the main bedroom; here again, without pretense, exacting carpentry accommodates the many slight irregularities of the eight-sided floor. A low oak wall and bookshelf separates the stair from the bed. A curtain rail curves on the ceiling above, offering enclosure—what Tane calls a "soft division"—to the sleeping area. Eight niches are arrayed around the bed. One accommodates a Perriand sideboard, a clock and a Monstera philodendron; another contains a rush-seated reading chair. In a third, potted plants rest on a windowsill. A large window opens from each of these niches and, shifting with the geometry of the house, presents a different aspect of the tree canopy outside. Behind the bed and stair, through a glass wall, three more niches accommodate the bath and shower. Here too, the view carries past lush plants to the swaying tree branches. A built-in armoire occupies the seventh niche, and a beautifully crafted oak stair climbs within the eighth to more sleeping spaces above.

On the top floor is a single hexagonal room. Its soft divisions provide multiple sleeping arrangements for a growing family. Windows peer out over pitched rooftops, above the canopy of Todoroki Park, to distant high-rises. A door swings out to a small, thickly planted rooftop terrace over the entry court below. It is evident here why Saito says the house "gets along beautifully with the wind." The dry air blows, bringing with it the soft sounds of stirring leaves and also, quietly, almost forgotten, the noises of the city beyond.

Tane was only 26 when he won his first major project: a joint commission to design the Estonian National Museum.

Todoroki Valley is a tranquil, almost jungle-like neighborhood that feels a world away from central Tokyo.

FEATURES

The house is designed with floor-to-ceiling windows that connect it to the tropical vegetation that the valley is known for.

Le Chat Chic

Hey kitty girl! Join us in the studio with Socrate—the Parisian glamour puss who always lands on his feet.
Photography by *Luc Braquet* & Styling by *Tania Rat-Patron*

Previous spread: Socrate accessorizes with a Dior bracelet. Left: He throws caution—and a vintage Hermès silk scarf—to the wind.

Socrate sports a Polo Ralph Lauren pocket square and a jaunty beret from Laulhère Paris.

Socrate considers a purse from Domestique Paris. He wears his own fur coat.

THE INVENTION OF CHILDHOOD

TEXT:
KATIE CALAUTTI

What does it mean to be young? In agrarian societies, babies often weren't named until they were toddlers. Artists in the Middle Ages painted children as miniature adults (if they painted them at all). And the Victorians put them to work in coal mines. With help from historical treatises, children's books and Mister Rogers, Katie Calautti explains why "kids will be kids" has meant so many different things over the centuries.

In recent years, "intensive parenting" has replaced tiger moms and helicopter dads as the most talked about trend in child-rearing. Intensive parents don't just demand academic perfection and hover around in an effort to mitigate risk—they also plan their child's extracurricular activities down to the minute, play with them and encourage them to communicate about everything happening in their heads. Think: parent as professor, personal assistant, playmate, therapist and disciplinarian. And while some believe this approach paves a smoother path to success for little ones, others say it's robbing them of their self-reliance.

Experts lament the hothousing of childhood and the pressures placed upon the young right from birth. But when we decry childhood as "lost," what exactly are we referring to? The idea of life beginning with a period of carefree playfulness has, in fact, only recently been found. Perhaps it was even invented.

It all began with the 1960 release of *Centuries of Childhood: A Social History of Family Life* by French historian Philippe Ariès, a self-dubbed "anarchist of the right." His explosive stance—that, prior to the 17th century, childhood effectively didn't exist, and children were simply treated as small adults—ignited a firestorm of research by anthropologists, sociologists, behavioral psychologists and historians. This was the 1960s: the dawn of an era of political activism and reproductive freedom, of sex, drugs and rock and roll. The family unit was poised

to shift, but—according to a 2014 Council on Contemporary Families survey—in 1960, 65 percent of American children lived with married parents where the father worked and the mother stayed home. As such, it was a particularly loaded decade for a historian to claim that children had not always been uniquely nurtured, prized members of a family.

American children's book author Shel Silverstein once wrote, "There are no happy endings. Endings are the saddest part, so just give me a happy middle and a very happy start." He, like most children's authors, understood childhood in the way that has become commonplace in America: that children are the most valued members of society, and that the beginning of life should be a precious cocoon in which the child's every need is catered to. Anthropologist David F. Lancy coined a term for this approach: neontocracy. The opposite of this—and the more prevalent system, historically speaking—he calls a gerontocracy, which emphasizes its oldest members.

Lancy posits that gerontocracies approach children as "pick-when-ripe": they aren't fully recognized until they master adult actions and thinking. In neontocracies, children are "pick-when-green": personhood is recognized immediately, then carefully cultivated. And though most of the modern world is ruled by the urge to shape and speed ripening, history seems to suggest we should let nature take its course. As historian Peter N. Stearns puts it in *Grow-*

ing Up: The History of Childhood in a Global Context, children were considered "economic liabilities" in early human economies such as hunter-gatherer societies. Small children exercised autonomy—they weren't separated by age groups or sheltered from adult experiences. They learned by watching and exploring, and the parental approach was decidedly hands-off. A child walked too close to the fire and burned herself? She never did it again. He picked up a knife and cut himself? He quickly understood the meaning of the tool.

When societies transitioned to early agrarian economies, the difficulties of being a child doubled. Along with struggling to be fed and nurtured, they became an integral part of the workforce. Now, a family's worth and survival were dependent on how much land they had and the harvest it brought them—so children worked in the fields. These days, a five-year-old is relegated to playing with age-appropriate toys; back then, he would've been running atop newly seeded soil with drums to scare away birds, weeding, or helping with the harvest.

Before the advent of modern medicine and sanitation, mortality rates for children ranged from 30 to 50 percent; death was an expected quotient in the family planning calculation. As a result, infants were often left in a state of probation, not named until they were years old—and so likelier to go the distance—or instead bequeathed the monikers of their deceased siblings. Committing affection and resources to a child wasn't practical until its survival was guaranteed. And even when it was, surplus children were often abandoned, hired out or given to other families—anything to even out resources. Late-in-life children were afforded one new function, though: They were planned by parents so they could stick around and take care of them in their old age.

It wasn't until the Enlightenment that childhood as we know it found a foothold. Familial love and nurturing was officially in vogue and art reflected the changing attitudes toward children. "Childhood, like all the concepts that govern our sense of who we are, is constantly evolving," says Anne Higonnet, chair and professor of art history at Barnard College of Columbia University. "Artists are always trying to express the values of their moment." Whereas medieval works rarely pictured children (and if they did, they looked like small adults), works created during the Enlightenment celebrated children as individuals. Ariès notes an uptick in family portraits with children prominently displayed, underscoring their integral part in the unit. He also mentions a trend toward portraits of dead children, which rose as the infant mortality rate fell. Child death was becoming an exception instead of a rule and families valued lost children enough to commemorate them.

The 18th-century French artist Jean-Baptiste-Siméon Chardin was one of the first to focus on painting individual portraits of children as they now were: immersed in play. His thoughtful depictions of everyday actions—a child blowing a soap bubble through a straw, playing with a spinning top, dealing a deck of cards—contributed to the public perception of the young having an interior life. "Chardin not only represents children engaged in occupations specific to childhood—like playing games—but he shows them as middle-class children," explains Higonnet. "[They're] iden-

tified by new consumer goods invented in the years 1680 to 1720, like personal furniture and cotton clothes, which help us understand that childhood was a modern, European invention, a key aspect of the new individualism of the Enlightenment."

Literature, too, had a widespread effect, especially on the burgeoning idea of mass education. John Locke's An Essay Concerning Human Understanding (1689)—and specifically his tabula rasa or "blank slate" theory—was influential. "[It] popularized that we are all the products of our environments and the way we are nurtured, rather than being born with a particular personality," explains Matthew Grenby, professor of 18th-century studies at Newcastle University. "This argues for the importance of education as the thing that makes us what we are." Locke's groundbreaking theories carved out childhood as a time for becoming. "The possibility of raising oneself through learning and hard work was something that suggested the importance of investing in education," says Grenby, who cites the growth of children's literature as one example of this evolution.

Victorians, predictably, dressed this new idea of childhood up in some very pretty shapes, embracing what we know now as youth culture. They became obsessed with the cherubic vision of childhood, outfitting themselves in a manner that emphasized their youthful features. Children were primped to fit an androgynous ideal, becoming small pink-cheeked angels that parents increasingly looked to as sources of emotional comfort. Babies were paraded on the streets in bassinets, images of chubby, wide-eyed children were plastered on advertisements and in magazines, and child actors dominated stage performances.

But Victorian and Edwardian literature unearthed a wide rift between the reality and fantasy of childhood. At the time, many young victims of the Industrial Revolution worked in

> "When we decry childhood as 'lost,' what exactly are we referring to? The idea of life beginning with a period of carefree playfulness has, in fact, only recently been found."

perilous conditions at textile mills and coal mines or walked the streets in rags as hawkers. Charles Dickens and Elizabeth Barrett Browning described deplorable conditions plaguing poor children in Victorian-era cities. They were leading the way for greater understanding of class inequalities and, eventually, social reform and child labor laws. In her 1843 poem "The Cry of the Children," Barrett Browning wrote, "'For oh,' say the children, 'we are weary / And we cannot run or leap— / If we cared for any meadows, it were merely / To drop down in them and sleep.'" Meanwhile, J.M. Barrie, Lewis Carroll and many others spun a fanciful vision of childhood. As Peter Pan tells the children in J.M. Barrie's famous novel half a century later: "Even though you want to try to, never grow up."

Two World Wars swung the pendulum the other way, presenting a more somber picture of childhood. As in agrarian societies, death was at the forefront of a child's life; a famous World War I-era image shows a French child helping her mother in the kitchen while both wear gas masks—a disturbing juxtaposition of the mundane and the horrific that represents generations whose carefree youth was cut short. After the turbulence of war, 1950s America ushered in the short-lived invention of the traditional family: the white picket fence, the 2.5 kids, the mom who spends all day keeping house and has dinner on the table at 6 p.m. sharp, the dad who rushes in the door and stashes his briefcase just in time to sit down for grace. As social psychology professor Dr. Eli Finkel recently commented on the *Curiosity Podcast*, the purported domestic bliss of that decade was "an eye blink in history."

And then came Ariès, and our growing fascination with childhood development. The groundbreaking American children's television show *Mister Rogers' Neighborhood* hit national airwaves in 1968. Its compassionate

host struck a chord when he said to his audience, "There's no person in the whole world like you, and I like you just the way you are." *Sesame Street* followed the next year; it's now the most-watched children's educational television show in the world, reaching over 150 countries.

The culture of childhood was here to stay, but the commodification of it was just beginning. Stearns writes, "At some point in the twentieth century, parents in most places began to believe that providing goods and enjoyment to their children was a vital part of their role and began to experience real guilt when their capacity was inadequate." In sharp contrast to a time when people didn't even record their own ages (prior to the 18th century, Ariès notes, most did not care to know, let alone celebrate, this fact), the American song "Happy Birthday" has been translated and integrated into nearly every language. On a global scale, we've moved so far from medieval thoughts about age that we celebrate it once yearly, with much financial fanfare; the birthday party industry is a booming business. As Lancy writes, "Parenting has become the ultimate hobby."

"It was thought for a long time that children are incapable of many things," says Dr. Matt Johnson, professor of neuroscience at Hult International Business School. "That we need to have these certain things somehow encoded in our genetic endowment, and therefore it didn't really make a difference whether or not we interacted with children because they either had this compassion gene, or they had this personality or temperament gene, or language gene, or they didn't... it was all essentially predestined." But, on the heels of shifting attitudes after the Enlightenment, modern neurodevelopmental studies have firmly swung the pendulum the other way. "The emphasis is on learning. This led people to respond that yes, we actually do need to take care of these

little creatures. They are developing, and yes, genetics is important. But how we care for them, and how we include them in our family, and how we interact with them generally really has a massive effect on their long-term outcomes."

Children living in the first world are often coddled to the point of barely leaving the house, based on an array of parental fears. Computers and televisions have become a secondary caretaker; toys and technology are compensation for the lack of freedom. Alongside this commodification of childhood comes the phenomenon of prolonged adolescence: Demographers have identified a new group of "emerging adults," who rely on their parents well into their 20s. Meanwhile, many children in the developing world still struggle to survive. The technology held in one child's hands has been assembled by those of another in a far different society.

As many societies classify children by ages and abilities, sheltering them from experiences, providing largely impractical toys that are regulated by age appropriateness and curating their education—sometimes even before they're born—it can seem like we're moving further away from allowing children to explore and understand the tools they'll be using for the rest of their lives.

Was childhood as we currently know it invented by any one society? Its roots seem to have sprouted in 17th-century Europe; sometime in that era, children moved from the outside of the circle of family life to its center. "Everyone tends to believe that ideas as deep as childhood are forever ideas. But really, even the most basic ideas about how to organize society keep on changing," says Higonnet. From hands-off to helicoptering, maybe society's latest parenting innovation is manufacturing needs to replace fundamental requirements. Only time, a host of attentive experts and legions of intensive parents, will tell.

Ahead of

A playful guide to making your carry-on less of a carry on. Photography by Zoltan Tombor

the Pack

Set Design by Áron Filkey

Though we favor packing light, we do not take packing lightly. For the summer holidays, *Kinfolk* partners with Totokaelo and folds essential pieces from Totokaelo Archive's thoughtfully assembled new collection into our hand luggage.

Left: Cardigan sweater by Totokaelo Archive. Above: Scarf by Pleats Please Issey Miyake. Previous spread: Luggage by Rimowa and sneakers by Common Projects.

Mock neck sweater, crew neck sweater and top by Totokaelo Archive, bag by Homme Plissé Issey Miyake, Oxford shirt by MM6 Maison Margiela and sunglasses by Celine.

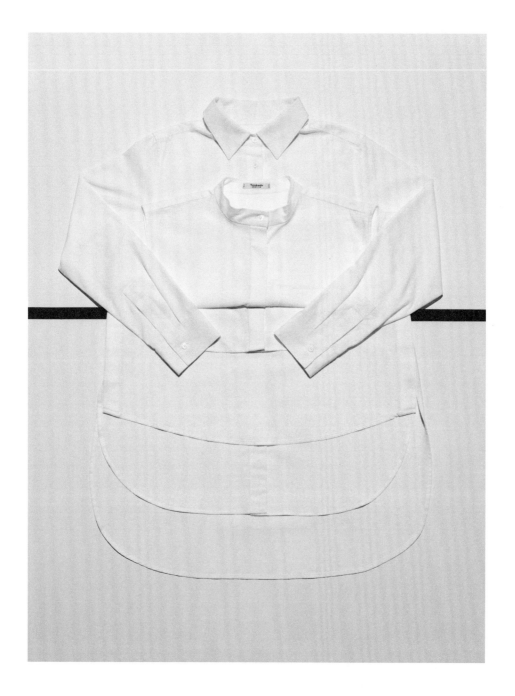

Above: Shirt and sleeveless top by Totokaelo Archive. Right: Straight leg trousers by Totokaelo Archive.

Robe coat by Totokaelo Archive.

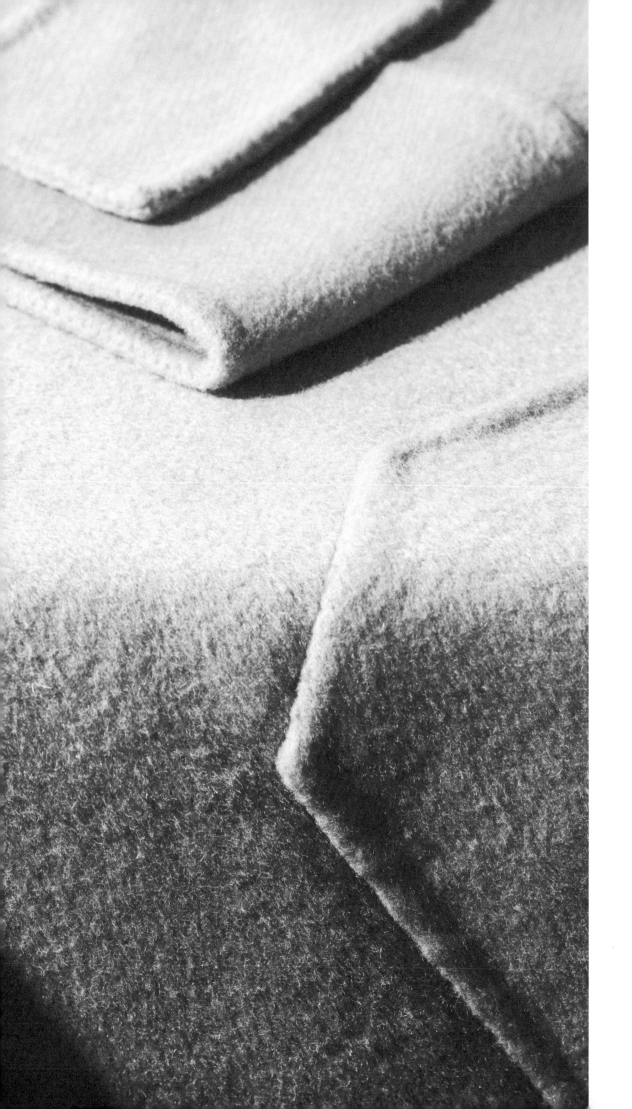

All clothing by Totokaelo Archive.

3
Tokyo

Y O

Meet the designer who made Tokyo her home, then took the city's grunge-chic aesthetic to Dior—and the world.

A H

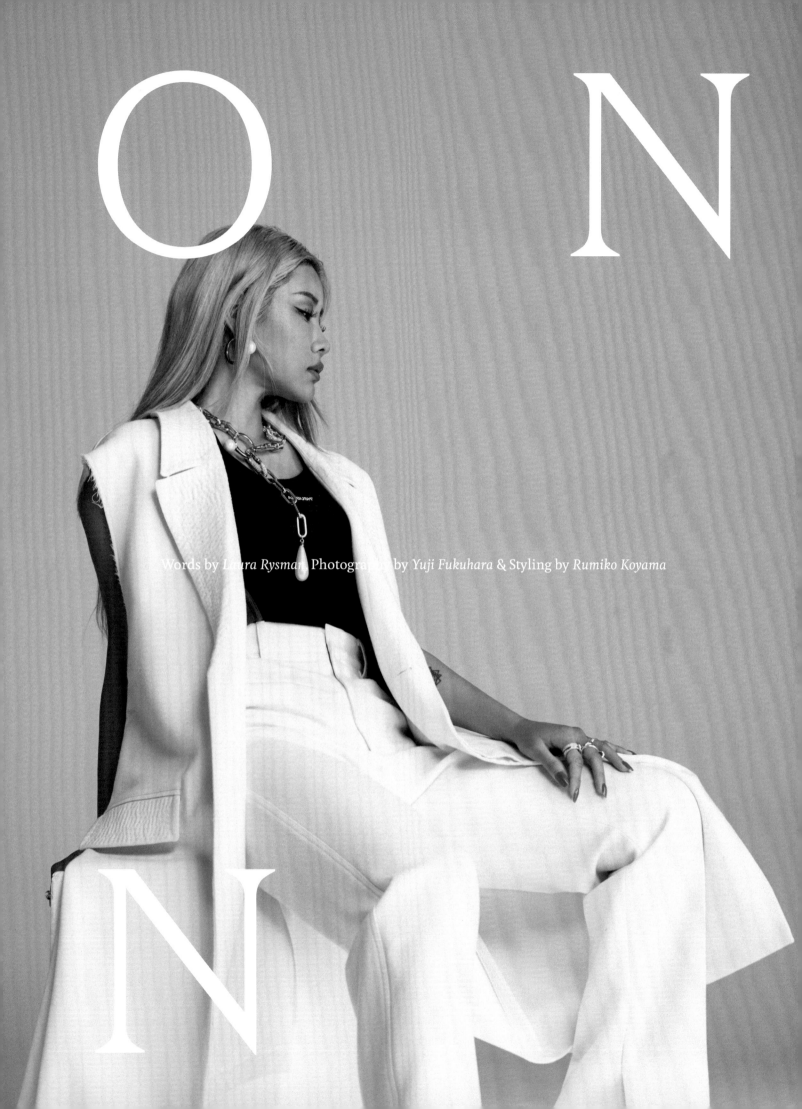

O N

Words by *Laura Rysman*, Photography by *Yuji Fukuhara* & Styling by *Rumiko Koyama*

N

"I really love this city. Tokyo is always moving, always shifting."

"Everything in life is always preparing me for something bigger," says the designer Yoon Ahn, tying back her mermaid-length champagne-blond hair, and settling into a chair after wrapping up a morning photo shoot. She has just flown back home to Tokyo from a family trip to Honolulu—a rare vacation in a calendar that keeps the 41-year-old traveling the world. Along with her commitments to Ambush—her phenomenon of a streetwear brand—she has countless collaborations and a post since last year as Dior Homme's jewelry designer. To the highly determined Ahn, achievements stack like a ladder to be climbed.

Born in Korea, raised in the Seattle suburbs and a graduate of Boston University, Ahn moved to Tokyo in 2003 with the rapper Verbal (real name Young-Kee Yu), her future husband and partner at Ambush. She arrived not speaking Japanese, but 16 years later, there's nowhere she feels more at ease than in her 16th floor Shibuya apartment, or at the nearby Ambush studio, which sits above the brand's minimalist concrete flagship at street level. "I really love this city," she sighs. "Tokyo is always moving, always shifting, but the undercurrent of the country is so traditionalist, so it's an interesting intersection here." She sees the most rapid developments from her window, surveying the many cranes in action as the city prepares for the 2020 Olympics, but she embraces the possibilities of change. "It's exciting—it will bring more people to where I live, and even more energy." In fact, she's dedicating her next collection to the Tokyo Olympics.

Ahn and Verbal met at a local church while they were both students in Boston. Finding her way in Tokyo, a new and foreign city, she tried graphic design jobs and styling gigs, and then began designing showpiece jewels for Verbal to wear onstage, working with local goldsmiths to bring the pieces to life. "We had to," she explains. "You can always find any kind of clothes you want, but the jewelry wasn't out there, and jewelry is so personal, especially in rap culture, with their custom chains and stuff—it becomes like a person's logo."

From the sizable 18-karat showstoppers of Verbal's rap performances, Ahn started designing smaller pieces in humbler metals for people she knew. But the real groundswell began when Kanye West, a personal friend, sported Ahn's big, cartoon-style pavé-encrusted Pow! pendant necklace. The occasion presented a crossroads for Ahn and her fledgling project: She could fritter away the fervor around her hobby, or take the leap and become an entrepreneur heading up a genuine brand. By 2008, Ambush was born, and Ahn was navigating the market.

"People don't realize that a brand is beyond just designing. You're the leader of a business and you have employees," she says. "I think the real creativity is in how you construct your business." Certainly, Ahn has managed to craft a trailblazing company whose products are smartly tailored to an eager slice of the public.

"In the earlier stages, I used to make crazier pieces, but they don't sell," she says coolly, pursing her scarlet-painted lips. As she talks, she packs up long bundles of the blond weave she wore for her shoot, combing out each one with her stiletto-sharp crimson nails. Her high-impact look—on this day, a crisp white sweatshirt and a gemstone-studded choker chain encircling the base of her neck; on all days, layers of Ambush

Ahn wears a vest coat, tank top, trousers and jewellery by Ambush.

"It doesn't get any more Shibuya than me... the clubs, the culture, I've lived all of that."

gear and extravagant makeup—has made her the prime avatar of her
own brand. Ahn's online identity—she has almost 400,000 Instagram
followers—has become as fundamental to her line as the apparel itself.

"What makes a great designer is being able to come up with something creative but also make it desirable for a great number of people,"
says Ahn. "I get more creative when I know my boundaries." That clear-
sighted approach rendered her a 2017 finalist in the LVMH awards, and
helped her guide Ambush through a wealth of collaborations ranging
from Chitose Abe of Sacai, to Nigo of A Bathing Ape, and Jun Takahashi
of Undercover. She also designed a celebrated collection of Nike athlet-
ic gear sharp enough for the club, and military-inspired sneakers for
Converse that were an instant sensation. There are upcoming projects
as well—a Nike World Cup collection in June, Gentle Monster sunglasses in July, plus "a lot I can't announce."

For Ambush, Ahn oversees both the creative and business direction, while Verbal handles the administrative side. Since adding a clothing line in 2015, she's proven adept at reimagining sports styles into
genre-defining must-haves, from her sleek (and fully functional) white
wetsuit to futuristic takes on military jackets inspired by David Bowie in
The Man Who Fell to Earth. The jewelry that established Ahn's reputation
similarly remixes familiar items, turning the quotidian into something
distinctively uncanny: A faceless watch becomes a bracelet, a gold-plated
USB key becomes a pendant, a clothespin becomes an earring. They are
easy to sport yet loud and identifiable, instantly signaling a wearer's al-
liance with the international adherents of Ambush.

Since her appointment in April 2018 at Dior, Ahn has infused the
fashion house's jewelry for men with similar Instagram-ready recogniz-
ability, with logo-heavy pieces that resonate more with a hip-hip aesthetic than the classically restrained world of the Paris fashion house. Ahn,
who has never studied fashion or jewelry, sees the role at Dior—her first
official job in fashion beyond her own brand—as less complicated than
heading up Ambush, where she compares her responsibility to that of
Christian Dior himself. "Mr. Dior was there for nine years and created
all the codes, then you have decades of designers reworking that heritage," she says. "I don't know if Ambush is going to carry on for 60 or
70 years, but I have to create the DNA, I have to create all the codes. At
Dior, all the codes are there, so it's easier for me."

Yet this is a time when the codes of Dior, and many other high fashion
houses, are shifting radically, and Ahn herself is a potent symbol of that
change. A self-taught designer who is Tokyo-based, Asian and female, she
is bringing the democratized and global aesthetic of streetwear to the couture house and breaking into a realm traditionally dominated by European
men with institutional pedigrees and a rarefied vision of couture luxury.

Ahn's appearance at Dior was part of a chain reaction. In March 2018, Dior hired Kim Jones—a designer noted for imparting a streetwear-friendly aesthetic to the runway in his former position at Louis Vuitton—to direct the menswear line. Jones then hired Ahn—the two had been friends for over a decade. To underscore the new guard's arrival at Dior, Jones brought in the street artist KAWS, who collaborated on designing a selection of pieces. For Jones' inaugural show, KAWS even designed a 30-foot-high sculpture of a besuited version of his BFF character, crafted with 70,000 flowers. (The show ended with Jones taking his lap around the runway leading Ahn by the hand.) Extraordinary flower installations have been a part of Dior's runway sets since Raf Simons used them to create poetic hanging gardens and dense, romantic walls of flowers. KAWS' giant bloom-covered cartoon figure showed that Dior's elegant materials and craftsmanship would remain under Jones, but the outcome would be something far less reverent.

At the same time that Jones and Ahn started at Dior, Virgil Abloh was appointed to take over Louis Vuitton. Abloh—a friend of Ahn's and also an untrained designer (holding instead a degree in architecture)—had become one of the most blazing names in fashion with his own Off-White line. "People like me and Virgil, we don't come from the usual background of graduating from fashion school and getting our start as a fashion assistant," says Ahn. "Life was our school."

"I was intimidated when Kim invited me to come work at Dior," she continues. "But when I didn't know anything about business, I had to turn into a businesswoman. I had to come out with designs that made sense. That's more real than anything like fashion school." According to Ahn, her market-savvy experience with her own brand taught her how the commercial world functions, how to work with manufacturers and how to deal with retailers and clients. "It's natural that I'm in this position because I'm fit for it," she says. "What do I bring to Dior Men? What's modern, what's 2019, what people actually want to buy."

So far in her tenure with Dior, that's meant more pop style from the Tokyo streets than Paris couture, but this is the sea change that Ahn is helping to foment. Making the commute back to Tokyo helps keep her design roots and her personal voice vital, maintaining a connection to the city that fostered her original ideas in the aughts when she was part of the vibrant local club scene.

"In club culture you have to get dressed up to stand out," she says, comparing the eccentricity of the period to the dynamism of London club life in the 1980s and '90s. Her taste for extreme looks solidified in those days, after years of being more muffled in the tamer environs of Boston and Seattle. The immersion into Tokyo's club tribes would influence the iconography of her designs, with her references to surfers, grunge kids, bikers, high school misfits and more. "It wasn't like the US where everyone who goes to a particular club dresses the same way and listens to the same music," she says. "Some people were punk, some people were hip-hop, but everyone was gathered in one room." It was a time of endless parties and she met "everyone in the fashion industry that way," she says. "That's how a lot of my early collaborations came about—very organically, because of human relationships."

Those relationships established her home among this city of 20 million. "From the outside looking in, Tokyo seems crazy," she says. "But living here, everyone knows each other in the fashion community—it's quite a tight group of people."

Ahn has lived in the same high-rise for 13 years, at the center of Tokyo's most boisterous, youthful neighborhood, Shibuya—the heart of nightlife in the world's most populous city. "It doesn't get any more Shibuya than me. I've seen all the changes. There's so much that came in here, the clubs, the culture, and I've lived all of that," she says. The area is less popular as a residence for foreigners, but Ahn no longer feels like one in any case. "I'll never fully become Japanese because I grew up elsewhere," she says. It was her father's position in the military that moved her family between South Korea, Seattle, Hawaii and California. "But this is my home. It's just that my outlook is much wider than people who never left their country."

It's an outlook that's in continual evolution. Ahn no longer frequents Tokyo's clubs. "Maybe I'm jaded," she says. "But I don't feel like there's a scene worth checking out anymore." Instead, before packing in a 12-hour day (still shorter than it used to be) at the Ambush office, she diligently gets up at four or five in the morning "when everything is silent except for my cats," and spends a couple of hours reading and contemplating design, turning to books and creations from the past instead of the electric energy of club life for inspiration.

"Working at Dior really changed me because I started to think about legacy and making something that could be more lasting," she says. "So I look at art, furniture and architecture that stand the test of time after 40 or 50 years," trying to understand "what about the piece still makes sense in the 21st century."

With her own work—cassette tape earrings, padlock chokers, lighter holders as pendants—she seeks to transpose the prosaic into eloquent new forms. "I want to give value to things that people overlook," she says. "Part of the designer's job is to make people look at things in a new way." For Ahn, at this pinnacle in her ambitious career, a fanatical crowd awaits whatever she wants to show them next.

"What do I bring to Dior Men? What's modern, what's 2019, what people actually want to buy."

Ahn wears a trench coat, shoes, necklace and keyring by Dior and earrings by Ambush. All rings by Dior.

Tokyo

As daylight fades into the neon lights of night, Tokyo reflects its own glow.

Rising

Photography by Romain Laprade & Styling by Daisuke Hara

Left: Hiromi wears a jacket and shirt by Yohei Ohno and a skirt by John Lawrence Sullivan. Above left: She wears a top by Jens and a skirt by Hyke. Above right: She wears a top and shorts by Hermès. Previous spread: See Credits on page 191.

Below: Keisuke wears a jacket and shirt by Hermès. Right: Hiromi wears a jacket and skirt by Yohji Yamamoto.

Above left: Keisuke wears a jacket and shirt by Issey Miyake Men. Above right: He wears a suit by John Lawrence Sullivan. Right: He wears Issey Miyake Men head-to-toe.

Below: Hiromi wears a coat by Hermès. Right: Keisuke wears a suit by John Lawrence Sullivan and a shirt by Yuki Hashimoto.

東京無線3852

Above: Hiromi wears a dress by Hyke and a slip dress by Mister It. Right: Keisuke wears a jacket by Yuki Hashimoto, a shirt by Issey Miyake Men and trousers by Jens.

Archive:
Toko Shinoda

Nick Narigon profiles the centenarian artist who married calligraphy with Tokyo's post-war avant garde to become one of the most important abstract expressionists of her generation.

The prevailing theory of modern and contemporary art is that influence flows from West to East. The life and legacy of Toko Shinoda—who turned 106 this year—is a riposte to this, and much else besides. Her Sumi ink paintings hang in the most important museums in the world and belong in collections owned by the imperial family of Japan and the Rockefellers of New York. "I grew to admire Shinoda immensely, especially the way in which she balanced simplicity and strength," David Rockefeller once wrote. "Her art had a distinctiveness and power of its own, and was in no way derivative."

Today, Shinoda still lives in central Tokyo. She is deaf, and doesn't conduct interviews. Not confident in her memory, she has also stopped publishing essays. But she still paints: the same soaring abstract works that first made her a global name in the 1950s.

Shinoda was born in 1913 into a prominent Japanese family, and art played a central role in her Tokyo upbringing from an early age. Her great-uncle carved the personal seal of Emperor Meiji and her father zealously pursued calligraphy and Chinese poetry. Calligraphy lessons for his daughter began at age six, and the art form became the framework for her life's work: her teacher's red correction marks later became a signature part of her style.

"The teacher's red Sumi sometimes overlapped and sometimes sharply swerved from the strokes of the letters I had drawn," Shinoda later recalled. "Occasionally, I thought the vermilion shades fascinating. Not a model student, however, I often inwardly rebelled against the intruding red." (Now a former calligraphy teacher herself, people sometimes ask Shinoda why she no longer takes students. "Picasso didn't," is her retort.)

Shinoda's talent for calligraphy and her ability to network among Tokyo's high society led to her first solo exhibition in 1940 at a prestigious gallery in Ginza. Then World War II intervened. The American fire raids forced her family to flee to the countryside. Cash held no value, so they traded their fine kimonos and Tokugawa porcelain for rice and vegetables.

When Shinoda returned to American-occupied Tokyo, she found a city in upheaval. For the first time, citizens were allowed to rebel against authority, and Shinoda was in a good position to take advantage: Japanese women of her era were subject to their families, unable to divorce and often forced to raise children carried by their husband's mistresses. Shinoda, however, was unmarried and would remain single for life—citing her devotion to her artwork as her reason for never pursuing romance. Avant-garde schools of art popped up throughout the city, and Shinoda became increasingly involved with the creative scene. By the 1950s she had shed formal calligraphy altogether and was exclusively producing abstract paintings with Sumi ink.

Around that time, a curator from New York's Museum of Modern Art came to Tokyo seeking Japanese architects. Instead, he discovered calligraphy—and Shinoda. Her work was displayed at the museum in an exhibition of contemporary Japanese calligraphy in 1954 and, two years later, she decided to travel to America in person. With her brother's influential friend serving as financial guarantor, and a letter of recommendation from the director of the Tokyo National Museum of Modern Art in hand, Shinoda arrived in New York in 1956, at age 43, with a three-month visa.

She looked first to the expat community: from her hotel, she telephoned the abstract artist Kenzo Okada, who had left Japan six

The American art critic John Canaday once wrote of Shinoda's work "It is a rare artist whose modernism is rooted in tradition without compromise in either direction."

"Okada asked, 'Are you good?' Shinoda replied, 'I think so.'"

"She still holds the brush the same way she was taught 100 years ago."

years earlier. Okada asked, "Are you good?" Shinoda replied, "I think so."

Okada introduced Shinoda to gallery owner Betty Parsons, an early supporter of the new wave of abstract expressionist artists like Jackson Pollock, whose work Shinoda admired. Under her dealer's tutelage, Shinoda's career accelerated: she displayed her work in Boston, Cincinnati and Chicago. She struggled with English however, and with the weather. When producing art at her New York abode, she ran the shower and closed all the windows to increase the humidity. Still, the Sumi ink dried too fast on the washi paper. After two years of renewing her visa every few months, she returned to Tokyo.

When she landed at Haneda Airport, photographers and journalists were waiting to meet the Japanese lady who had made a name for herself in America. Unfortunately, art dealers were not. Eiji Nagao, senior advisor at the Tolman Collection, recalls frustrated conversations with the artist. "Toko told me once or twice, 'Nagao-san, today I

am somehow recognized by even young people, but in those days it was really difficult to sell my work,'" he recalls. She continued, disparagingly: "What's art in Japan? It's the tea ceremony goods. Tea bowls, the teaspoon made of bamboo or the hanging scroll. [Japanese collectors] pay a lot of money for those antique pieces, but not modern paintings."

Shinoda decided to broaden her palate. She began making lithograph prints, and became a celebrated essayist. She designed her own kimono, wearing her obi belt low on her hips the way men did during the days of the samurai.

Her art career was boosted when Japanese architect Kenzo Tange, the influential designer of the Hiroshima Peace Memorial Museum, tapped her to produce murals for his projects, including the Yoyogi National Stadium, built for the 1964 Tokyo Olympics. In 1974, she created a 92-foot-long mural for Zojoji, the 400-year-old temple revered by the Tokugawa shogunate. By the late 1970s, she was consid-

ered one of the key pioneers of abstract painting in Japan.

Those who met Shinoda during her most active period recall a steadfast, somewhat standoffish, master of her craft. Norman Tolman, the founder of the Tolman Collection and Shinoda's principal dealer for 40 years, remembers meeting the artist in the elevator of his Tokyo apartment building by coincidence. Tolman offered the small woman greetings, but she merely turned her cheek. When Tolman finally met Shinoda formally, he asked why she had given him the cold shoulder. "She said, 'I was brought up to never speak to anyone to whom I have not been properly introduced,'" says Tolman.

Eventually, Shinoda agreed to give the burgeoning art connoisseur the proverbial keys to her career, and he bought her to new markets as diverse as Finland and China. In 1996 she was the first Japanese artist to hold a retrospective at the Singapore Art Museum.

Last winter, Tolman and Nagao visited Shinoda at her central Tokyo

home. Nagao says he peeked inside her studio and saw artwork in progress. "For her, living is working," he says. "She said one of the secrets of her longevity is going to Yamanaka in the summer to get away from Tokyo heat, and the other is living on the third floor and the fourth floor, going up and down the stairs."

"If you look at her work from the very beginning and to the work she does right now, she knows what she wants to do," says Tolman. "In her mind, the painting has already been made. All she has to do, she says, is transfer what's in her head to the paper."

She still picks up the brush and holds it the same way she was taught 100 years ago, and will continue to do so for as long as she is able. "I still believe that the red of the setting sun and deep crimson of flowers can be expressed through the medium of Sumi ink," Shinoda once wrote. "However, the method by which that is done is a profound one, and one that cannot be arrived at during the course of a single lifetime such as my own."

Seven Cuts

Set Design: Andreas Frienholt

An umbrella. An octopus. A mask. A city seen through still life portraits. Photography by *Gustav Almestål*

Stacking tumblers are a neat storage solution. At the opposite end of the practicality spectrum, Ramune bottles double as a children's game thanks to their marble stopper.

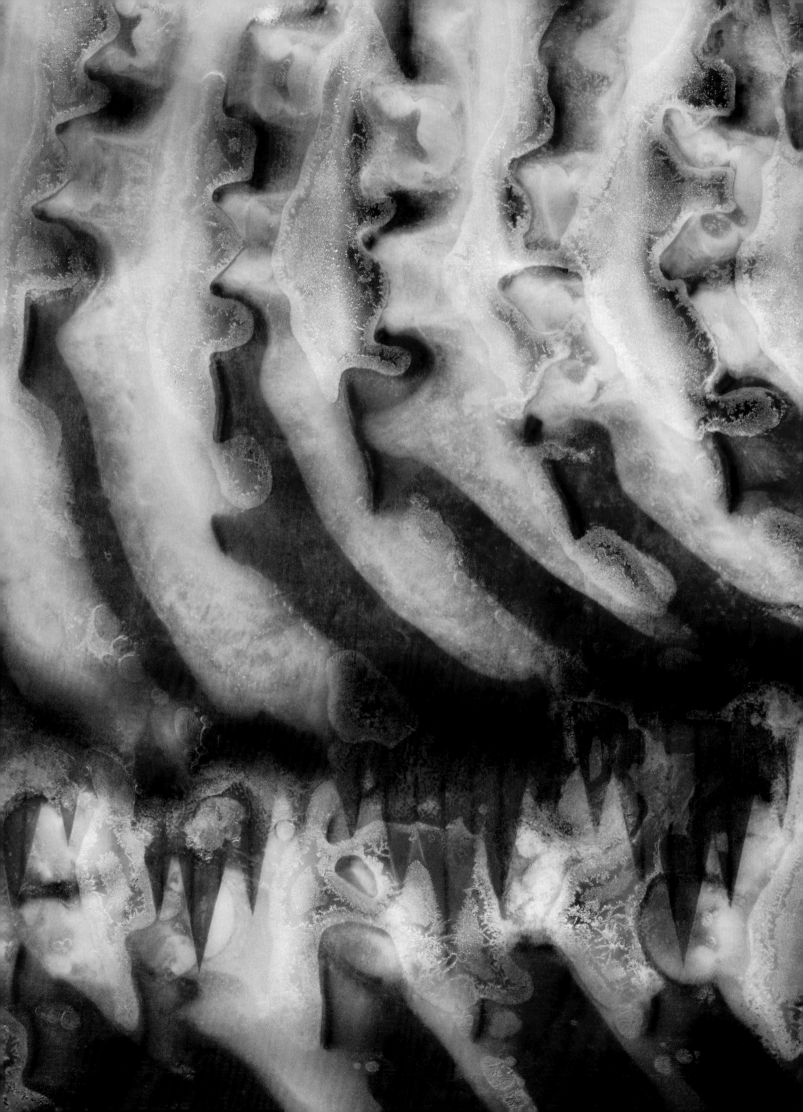

Who invented the sheet mask? Although the modern version originated in Korea it has early precedents in Japan, where geishas would soak kimono silk in flower water.

APOCALYPSE NEXT

TEXT:
MOEKO FUJII

Why is Tokyo the canvas for so many disaster fantasies? Moeko Fujii, who grew up doing regular earthquake drills at her school in Shibuya, looks back at the natural catastrophes, man-made crises and exoticizing impulses that made Tokyo the go-to "dystopian garnish" for generations of artists and filmmakers.

When I was a teenager living in Tokyo, I was told to imagine a dystopia for homework. I wrote a Japanified *Handmaid's Tale*, where women were mandated to fully concentrate on their biological functions. I included a scene in which teenage girls in classrooms fed robot babies, while a metallic voice on an intercom told them that they were "baby-making machines." This was an actual quote by Japan's health minister in 2007, I commented, in a heavy-handed footnote. I handed it in, then forgot about it.

My school was in between Shibuya and Harajuku, which was as central Tokyo as you could get. The building was designed to be earthquake-proof; L-shaped and extra-bendy, it was supposed to absorb shockwaves better. When we did earthquake drills, we would rip into the emergency kits, snap open the aluminum-foil blankets and wrap them around our bodies like capes, giggling. As we opened these packages, the instruction leaflet advised us to avoid being near buildings, that it was better to be in an open field. The irony that our school was in a high-rise building was not lost on us. Our teachers told us that we should hide underneath a table instead of running outside, where glass shards and billboards could fall from above.

When the Tohoku earthquake and tsunami hit in 2011, I was sick at home. My best friend texted me photos of our peers sleeping on the floor of our school, cocooned in those same aluminum foil capes. The trains weren't running, she explained: There was no way to get

home. A month later, I went to volunteer in the tsunami-ravaged regions in the north of Japan. I saw crumpled cars layered like Lego, buses that, swept up by a wave, now balanced on top of buildings. There it was, actualized: the destruction that always seemed to hover in our peripheral vision as a possibility during my teen years in Tokyo.

Is there any city more inextricably linked to ruin than Tokyo? It has long been the canvas for projections of a dystopian future. In the city's beginnings in the early 17th century, when it was called Edo, a girl named Yaoya Oshichi burned the city down for love. Oshichi, or so the story goes, met a handsome temple page during one of the many great fires of the period. Consumed by desire and convinced that the only way she could see him again was through another great fire, she decided to light a match. She was soon aflame on a stake, burned for the crime of arson. I've always been drawn to woodcut prints depicting the story, showing Oshichi looking down at the crackling city. Was it longing for a boy she had met once, or was it awe at the scale of destruction that she—a 16-year-old greengrocer's daughter—could wreak in the name of love? In those early prints, devastation was already an aesthetic. Tokyo burned as a metaphor for the dangers of unbridled desire.

Tokyo's association with disaster has long been fodder for the artistic imagination, but it is grounded in fact. Consider the city's many historical ravishments: the Great Kanto Earthquake of 1923, depicted by Hayao Miyazaki in

The Wind Rises as a bellowing, rippling roar that flung houses into the air at high noon. Or the Great Tokyo Air Raid in 1945, when the United States dropped 1,665 tons of bombs on the city in a single night. Or the Aum Shinrikyo attacks in 1995, in which cult members released sarin gas in the Tokyo subways. The death count was a dozen—tiny, compared to the catastrophes that preceded it—but it terrorized a nation that had started to forget how it felt to be under attack.

Given a decent imagination, this storm of domestic, foreign and cosmic forces can spiral to an infinity of apocalyptic futures: Tokyo burns, Tokyo falls, Tokyo reemerges.

It's no surprise that the king of monsters was born here. Since it first emerged from Tokyo Bay in 1954, Godzilla—or as it's known in Japan, Gojira—has appeared in nearly three dozen film renditions. "Other global cities, even ones with histories of destruction—San Fransisco and the earthquake, Chicago and the fire, London and its fire, as well as the World War II Blitz—have just never attracted such intense disaster fantasies," says William Tsutsui, president of Hendrix College—and a Godzilla scholar.

I like our king of monsters. I like how, in my favorite Godzilla movies, he never really makes it about himself. Godzilla is inscrutable and unpredictable, and in director Hideaki Anno's *Shin Godzilla* (2016), he is a huge, 150-foot prompt for widespread terror, and the subsequent need for a capable government response. He is powered by nuclear radiation, and thus the film is punctuated by politicians hurriedly assuring the public that "the radiation level is not too high, yet." This feels oddly familiar to Japanese viewers, as it should: The film is a spot-on satire of the Japanese government scrambling blindly in the wake of the March 2011 earthquake and tsunami. "It's not an earthquake, nor a typhoon," a politician points out in *Shin Godzilla*. "It's a living organism. That means we should be able to stop it."

Godzilla is man-made (most Godzillas are men in latex suits) and yet larger than man: His unexpected arrival prompts us to wrestle with what the response should be—what laws we should cling to—when we are faced with something even more threatening than a terrorist attack or a climate catastrophe. All states of emergency highlight the deficiencies of any bureaucratic and political system, and the failure of manners—not the monster—is at the heart of the film. After being commanded to do as much research as possible to capture the monster, as quickly as possible, a group of wan, gray-haired bureaucrats glance at each other, furtively. One asks: "Excuse me: Which government office did you allocate that to?"

I love how revealingly finicky Godzilla is. In his destruction of Tokyo, he will topple the Tokyo Tower, blaze through the Diet Building and kill most of parliament, but he won't ever step on the Yasukuni Shrine, or squat on the Imperial Palace. I also like how, as Tsutsui told me, he's grown taller over the years, expanding to match the rising skylines of Japanese cities. He's been foe and friend, and back again, but the fascination hasn't ceased. "We have now seen a big reptile destroy Tokyo in much the same way almost three dozen times, and yet we happily come back for more whenever a new sequel is released," Tsutsui says. He points out how fitting it is that at the end of *Shin Godzilla*, the monster is frozen with a chemical liquid and turned into a giant statue right next to Tokyo Station. Godzilla literally becomes part of the Tokyo skyline.

Tokyo is also the capital of tech dystopias, thanks mainly to cyberpunk—the genre of sci-fi futures in which technological advancements are juxtaposed against societal breakdowns. As we clocked in 2019 at a party in New York, an American friend reminded me eagerly that we were now squarely in the year of *Blade Runner*. "Wasn't that, like, set in Tokyo?" he asked. As I shook my head, another friend insisted that it was, in fact, set in a postmodern fusion of cities—a San Francisco-Tokyo hybrid. They were both wrong: It was set in Los Angeles, but a Los Angeles overlaid with the Tokyo-as-aesthetic, Tokyo-as-detail cyberpunk vision. For director Ridley Scott, Tokyo was the city of chrome, holograms, grunge and bonsai—the neon inspiration behind a now-dated prophecy that Japan would become a global superpower, the US would lag behind, and there'd be a knotty relationship with technology and robots.

I wish I could say that I hadn't liked cyberpunk as much as I did, that I hadn't torn through the sci-fi novels of William Gibson as a teenager, sitting on the carpeted floor of a bookstore in Shinjuku. But I had. Once upon a time, I'd luxuriated in the way in which Japanese seemed to breed with ease with the English language in Gibson novels—*sarariman, gaijin, idoru*—words used without clunky definitions or italics, sentences that seemed to demand a reader familiar with Japanese. In Gibson's imagination, the slow, aging suburb I lived in was Chiba City, said with a hush, where things happened in the dystopian underworld. There was an egotism to my liking it, as well as a skewed feeling of being seen, for where were the Japanese names in Penguin Classics? The realization that Gibson used Tokyo as dystopian garnish, that Japanese names were used for exotic one-note effect, that Chiba could've been called Hakone, or Tsukiji, or anything that "sounded Japanese"—would come later.

Blade Runner's core themes are about identity—is Deckard a robot, or human? And thus, the film's conspicuous lack of Asian bodies is more

"Once we wipe the neon smog from our eyes, we are left with some questions. How much of the dystopian menace of *Blade Runner* is due to the alien feel of a future in which bilingual neon kanji signs and Japanese ads flash in every corner of an American city?"

than a little jarring. Once we wipe the neon smog from our eyes, we are left with some questions. How much of the dystopian atmosphere is attributed to the threat of the robot-replicants, and how much of the menace is due to the alien feel of a future in which bilingual neon kanji signs and Japanese ads flash in every corner of an American city?

Blade Runner was released on June 25, 1982. Just two days before, two white autoworkers had clubbed Vincent Chin, a Chinese-American, to death in Detroit. They'd thought he was Japanese. The shadows of the rhetoric they'd used— "It's because of you little motherfuckers that we're out of work"—is part of the malevolence of the world of *Blade Runner*. Fear and exclusion have always accompanied the development of machines and technology: Who gets to create and control them, and who will guard the guards? This injects a particular kind of menace to the idea that is a core of cyberpunk, to the idea of Tokyo-as-dystopia.

Today, there are no cartwheeling robots, but the imagined worlds that still make up the stuff of films—think Scarlett Johansson, or other white characters, walking around an aestheticized landscape that evokes Tokyo as garnish, and possibly, as threat—are hardly different.

Six years after *Blade Runner* was originally released, a Japanese animator named Katsuhiro Otomo set his dystopian Tokyo in 2019, in an obvious homage to the film. *Akira*, however, starts 31 years after a nuclear bomb wiped out Tokyo, at the end of World War III. In this groundbreaking animated film, Neo-Tokyo— like today's Tokyo—is preparing for the 2020 Olympic Games. It's an errant thought, but one worth asking: Why do we thrill at the idea of reaching the year of dystopias? In the opening sequence, a boy in a red jumpsuit, Kaneda, tears forth on a red motorbike, his wheels snapping green hairs of electricity. He swings into the streets of Neo-Tokyo, filled with crushed cars. Skyscrapers seem to glow from within, blood-red and orange and sickening green, and an

Ebisu god chortles to himself in a hologram advertisement. Welcome to Tokyo, where the aesthetic is very much cyberpunk—but cyberpunk as envisioned by Katsuhiro Otomo, who was committed, as he said in a 1993 interview, to showing Tokyo as a character in the film.

"There's an oppressiveness about the way he angles his camera—we are constantly looking up," says Susan Napier, professor of rhetoric and Japanese at Tufts. "Only in animation can the city really be brought out as an entity in itself; it takes up the screen." Napier has long argued that animation's delight in highlighting the unreal and the unlikely makes it an ideal medium for science fiction and dystopias. She may have been talking about the body—in *Akira*, the antihero's body morphs and transforms in an unforgettably grotesque coda—but her idea can be applied to cityscapes, too. For the first 11 minutes of the film, we can't see the sky— every gap between buildings is filled with more buildings, and even when the camera pans up, we just see more skyscrapers. We are pushed up against an immense feeling of claustrophobia.

Dystopian and apocalyptic narratives often incorporate the idea that leaving is impossible. Tokyo's ambiguous boundaries, its never-ending-ness, particularly suits this theme. In apocalyptic films—like *Shin Godzilla*, for example—the first crisis is the airports shutting down, and then the trains, and then even car travel. Only Godzilla can go where he wishes, on his whim.

Susan Napier notes, "Tokyo is kind of this amorphous entity that you can project things onto." She adds that in the apocalyptic anime series *Neon Genesis Evangelion*, which is set in a city named Tokyo-3, the cityscape is also a generic, could-be-anywhere canvas; Mt. Fuji is much more prominent than the city itself. William Tsutsui agrees: "Considering that Tokyo does not have a well-defined or famous skyline, it's somewhat surprising to me that it has become such a favorite for apocalypse in a very visual age.

In *Akira*, power is projected onto the figure of the Colonel, a military man who alone has the mobility to traverse all of Tokyo, from the inner sanctums of parliament to the skies. He's committed to stopping those who might try to control the vast telekinetic force of a mysterious figure and usher in ruin. He can't. Tetsuo, the small, crouching antihero of the film—first introduced as a frail, low-level lackey in the motorcycle gang—finds himself controlling this growing telekinetic force. Like Yaoya Oshichi, the girl who burned Edo to the ground, we see Tetsuo stunned, and rather ecstatic, at the level of destruction his small body can wreak. This leads to a final showdown between the two at the newly built Olympic Stadium, which ends with the stadium—and most of Neo-Tokyo—swallowed into an orb of all-destroying white light.

And again, Tokyo falls. But Tokyo claps the dust of destruction off its knees, and gets up, as it always has, after the fires of Edo, after Godzilla's ruinous rampages. In the dystopian mirror of cyberpunk, Tokyo rebuilds and survives, at least until 2019. In the Tokyo Metropolitan Government's promotion for the upcoming 2020 Tokyo Olympics, we see the opening sequence of *Akira*'s Neo-Tokyo spliced with similar-looking buildings in the current skyline. The idea of ruin sells. A sanitized version of it, anyway. The promotional video cuts to a generic shot of fireworks, well before Neo-Tokyo erupts into flames. That, I can imagine Japanese politicians murmuring, would have been flirting a little too wildly with karma.

There's a scene in *Akira*, in which a scientist and the Colonel ride a glass elevator, looking out at Tokyo—a vast, complex and forbidding network of green neon. The scientist comments that he thought the Colonel had always hated the city, to which the Colonel responds: "The passion to build has cooled and the joy of reconstruction forgotten. Now it's just a garbage heap made up of hedonistic fools." "Yes," the scientist replies. "But you're still trying to save it."

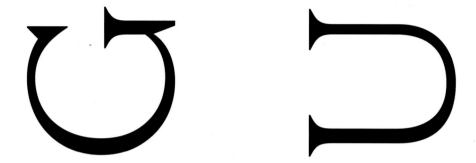

How do you navigate the world's most populous metropolis? With a guide that celebrates both heritage and innovation, and

I D E

crisscrosses neighborhoods to find the best examples of each. Words by Selena Hoy & Photography by Romain Laprade

Y O

1.

Takemura:

A family teahouse.

Built in the early Showa period, Takemura has been operating as a teahouse and sweetshop in the Kanda neighborhood since it first opened on January 25, 1930.

"The founder of this place was my father," says Masaaki Hotta, who is the third owner of the business following his father and older brother. The teahouse has always specialized in *oshiruko*—grilled mochi in a sweet adzuki bean soup. "My father was a *wagashi* [Japanese sweets] maker. At the start we served oshiruko and wagashi. However, during the war, sugar was really hard to come by, so at that time we were only open two or three days a week," Hotta explains.

The menu is a Japanese wagashi delight. In addition to the oshiruko, they serve *kuzumochi* (triangles of mochi made from kudzu starch), and other traditional favorites, all ready to be washed down with the plentiful green tea on offer.

Takemura's name reflects its materials. Literally meaning bamboo forest, it's a traditional wooden structure with a *kawara* tile roof, and bamboo accents throughout, including the low fence surrounding the building and structural elements on the sliding *shoji* screens. "This place has been serving oshiruko since its inception," Hotta says proudly. "This is the house-made specialty, so please try it when you stop by."

1-19 Kanda Sudacho
Chiyoda-ku
Tokyo 101-0041

2.
Higashiya Ginza:

A seasonal sweetshop.

In Ginza, where the streets are wide and the people polished, you'll find Higashiya Ginza—a shop and teahouse that makes fine *wagashi*, the refined confectionery that accompanies green tea in Japan. (The name Higashiya means "daily sweetshop.")

Each morsel offers no more than a few mouthfuls, though the diminutive bamboo picks with which they are served allow diners to stretch out the experience with tiny birdlike bites. In the adjoining café, diners can sample a wagashi flight with tea or liquor pairings. The confections change seasonally, but may include yuzu domyojikan, using citrus rind, agar and mochi rice; or the natsume butter sweet, which combines fermented butter, walnuts and date palm sugar.

The shop's design is the work of Shinichiro Ogata of Simplicity, and is as sophisticated as the treats it serves. Paulownia wood boxes tied with cord in precise stacks reach the ceiling, white hexagonal tiles brighten the floor and a white noren curtain at the entrance bears the shop's crest in red. The shape of the crest is also echoed in the door pull and the ceiling light molding, and on the round boxes that hold take-home treats.

Pola Ginza
Building 2F
1-7-7 Ginza
Chuo-ku
Tokyo 104-0061

3.

Asakura Museum of Sculpture:

7-18-10 Yanaka
Taito-ku
Tokyo 110-0001

A converted sculptor's studio.

Before it was a museum, the Asakura Museum of Sculpture was the home and studio of sculptor Fumio Asakura, who moved to the Yanaka area after graduating from Tokyo School of Fine Arts in 1907. He expanded the pwroperty over the years, completing a renovation in 1935 in order to open a sculpture school.

The current sprawling building was dedicated as a museum in 1967, three years after Asakura's death. It mixes Western styles—like the reinforced concrete, lofty ceilings and skylights of his studio—with the more traditional Japanese wooden structure where he lived with his family, like an enclosed garden and pond in the open-air center of the building. The living area, preserved with original furniture, offers an intimate look into the daily life of the artist.

Asakura's work, termed "objective realism," often reflected the character of the Yanaka neighborhood. His most famous work, *Hakamori*, or *The Grave Keeper*, was modeled on a man who worked nearby. The sculptor was also a cat lover, and frequently kept more than 10 cats at a time. Sculptures of his pets can be seen lounging and mincing around the museum, and are concentrated in the Orchid Room, a former hothouse.

4.

Morioka Shoten:

Suzuki Building 1F
1-28-15 Ginza
Chuo-ku
Tokyo 104-0061

A one-book shop.

Morioka Shoten literally means Morioka Bookstore and that's exactly what it is. Not, it should be noted, a *books* store; Morioka Shoten sells one book at a time.

Founder Yoshiyuki Morioka had the idea to launch the store when he attended a publishing event and noticed how many people came for just one book. "Publishers sold more books as a result. And I also sold more books. Readers and writers got to enjoy meeting," says Morioka. "There was this happy atmosphere around a single book. And, just with the one book, I felt like there was no need for any others." He opened Morioka Shoten in 2015.

The shop is a spare white room on a quiet street in the Ginza neighborhood. Pitted concrete walls are painted a smooth white, with windows at one end and an apothecary cabinet at the other. The book selection changes weekly, and the blank space makes a clean canvas for the revolving exhibit that accompanies each choice.

One week, the shop might resemble a Parisian chocolate shop as it displays a chocolate cookbook, while another week, the space is transformed into a tropical rainforest, based on a book about parrots. Morioka says, "While it often looks like a gallery from outside, the book is always absolutely at the center. And according to each book, the image here completely changes."

5.

Hoshinoya:

A modern *ryokan*.

From a distance, the building that houses Hoshinoya is another high-rise wrapped in glass and steel. Up close it's apparent that the steel facade is actually intricately patterned. "It's called *Edo komon*," explains Fumi Arai, a public relations manager at the hotel. "In the Edo period, commoners were not allowed to wear patterned kimonos, so they developed Edo komon." It's a tightly repeating pattern that looks solid from a distance but is discernible up close. "We are a *ryokan* [a traditional inn] in the financial district, and we're trying to blend in," he says.

Inside, Hoshinoya melds ryokan with luxury hotel. Elegant and spacious, its long expanses of chestnut paneled walls and spare decor are reminiscent of a Buddhist temple. Shoes come off at the entrance and are hidden away in bamboo boxes that seamlessly fade into the walls. The guest rooms mix low-slung Western furniture with tatami mats and sliding *shoji* panels. Privacy, quiet and comfort are overarching themes here. The ryokan only allows entry to its guests (this policy extends to the restaurant, which serves Japanese-French fusion cuisine). Each level, with its own dedicated staff and tea lounge, has six rooms and is exclusively accessible to guests staying on that floor. To complete the experience of secluded relaxation, the Hoshinoya pumps hot spring water from almost 5,000 feet deep for its penthouse hot spring bath, under an open skylight.

1-9-1 Otemachi
Chiyoda-ku
Tokyo 100-0004

6.

Mihoncho Honten:

A paper showroom.

Viewed from the street through its plate-glass window, the stark white interior of Mihoncho Honten looks almost clinical. Enter, though, and the waist-high display cases arranged in orderly rows and filled with sheets of paper in every hue, weight and texture imaginable, lend the shop more of a creative than cold atmosphere. This space serves as the showroom for Takeo, which has been making paper since 1899. The walls are stacked floor-to-ceiling with trays holding more samples; there are over 9,000 different papers in stock.

It's a dream destination for paper fans: Graphic designers, archivists, hobbyists and stationery enthusiasts flock here. Design is celebrated, and staff are on hand to offer advice on the right foil for a business card to catch the light, the best paper thickness to lend gravitas to a personal announcement, or the finest *washi* to add softness when bound into a book. In an increasingly digital world, Takeo focuses on the emotional connection that we have with paper and the way that its tactility appeals to the human senses.

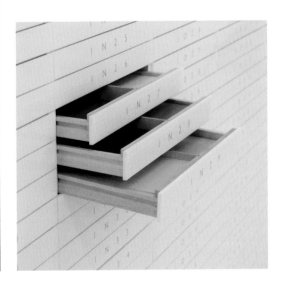

3-18-3 Kanda Nishikicho
Chiyoda-ku
Tokyo 101-0054

Yaeca Home Store:

4-7-10 Shirokane
Minato-ku
Tokyo 108-0072

A shop inside a home.

There's very little in the way of commerce near Yaeca Home Store in the upscale residential neighborhood of Shirokane. Located on a quiet street on a quiet hill, the concept shop is hidden behind the unmarked front door of a pretty but otherwise unremarkable house. Inside and to the right, a few pieces of handsome wooden furniture populate the living room. Vintage speakers pipe soothing, ambient music into the space. There are no price tags on anything.

In the kitchen, a woman behind glass is operating a KitchenAid mixer, and there's a tray of unbaked cookies on the counter in front of her. On a table on the other side of the glass, baked versions of the treats are neatly packaged in white wrappers and arranged in rows. Upstairs, in the bedroom, a few racks of black, white, camel and navy clothing stand in the center of the room. Made in Japan, the pieces are unisex and uniform. They reflect a minimalist but well-made aesthetic that matches the pared-down look of the rest of the house. A discreet curtain in the corner hides a single changing room. Less is more at Yaeca, and when less is beautiful and high quality, it is enough.

8.

Papier Labo:

A walk-in design studio.

At the edge of Harajuku is Papier Labo, a pint-sized art supplies shop and design office. Shelves are lined with art postcards, calendars and notebooks, along with house-designed bookends, limited edition bric-a-brac and old curios like vintage Japanese type blocks.

With a couple of hard-at-work designers sitting behind the counter and upstairs in the loft, the shop mainly serves as a small showroom for Papier Labo's own design and letterpress work. The designers here often collaborate with artists to create the original products on display, such as New Year cards for the 2019 zodiac year by woodblock artist Yuko Kan, or patterned cartons and illustrated stickers from artist Masanao Hirayama.

Papier Labo specializes in letterpress and embossing and can also produce engraved wooden and rubber stamps. The cash register doubles as a consultation desk where customers, after browsing the shop, can pore over paper samples and layouts with designers before placing an order for business cards, custom greeting cards or other items of stationery.

Beyond the requirements of individual customers, Papier Labo's designers also consult on graphic design and create logos and visual identities for other brands. Their clients include many local independent shops and businesses, but also bigger names like Stüssy and Beams.

4-8-6 Togoshi
Shinagawa-ku
Tokyo 142-0041

SyuRo:

A contemporary crafts shop.

The Torigoe neighborhood in Tokyo's Taito Ward has a rich history of craftsmanship that stretches back centuries. Metalworkers and makers of religious icons have long served the area's temples and shrines, and leather and textile workers have historically made a home here too. It's in this context that designer Masuko Unayama established SyuRo and began selling homeware that is functional and unfussy, and often made in the local area.

Housed in a former workshop, SyuRo resembles a gallery as much as a store. SyuRo's ethos rejects fast fashion and single-use products; materials such as linen and leather, stone and copper abound. The goods here take time and skill to make, and in turn, can be used for a long time. Carved wooden spoons and chopsticks are made from maple, Japanese oak and walnut. Square brass and copper cans are made by tucking and folding the metals, without soldering, to ensure they remain rust resistant. SyuRo also produces its own line of toiletries using organic oils like bergamot, sandalwood and vetiver in gender-neutral organic soaps, shampoos and moisturizers.

All of the products here are created or selected in accordance with monozukuri: the art of making things. These objects of beauty are to be used with love, treated well and used again and again.

1-16-5 Torigoe
Taito-ku
Tokyo 111-0054

10

1-2 Yotsuya,
Shinjuku-ku
Tokyo 160-0004

A classic *kissaten*.

The *kissaten* is Japan's answer to an American diner. The essential elements are coffee, stick-to-your-ribs food and a genial, homey atmosphere. Lawn in Yotsuya is a classic kissaten, the kind of place to smoke cigarettes and scribble in a notebook. There are no laptops in sight.

Hiroaki Ogura, the owner, has been serving up orders for a half century. "We opened in Showa 29—that's 1954," he says. "I took over the shop 10 years later, so I've been doing this for over 50 years."

Ogura is busy as he speaks, pouring coffee from a red enamel kettle with one hand, and melting butter in a pan with the other. The Beatles play on the stereo and cigarette smoke hangs in the air over the red vinyl booths. The kitchen is tiny, with a two-burner stove and just enough space for one chef. When he stands in the middle, Ogura can reach every corner. He starts making an omelet in the hot pan.

First-timers can't go wrong with an egg sandwich and a cup of strong coffee. "Since the beginning, we've sold these egg sandwiches. They're very popular," says Ogura, flipping the omelet. "I think the egg sandwich boom started here." His menu also offers thick slices of toast with jam or cheese. A few simple drinks like highballs and gin fizz round out the offerings.

11.

Okomeya:

A rice specialist.

Togoshi is a quiet neighborhood. Although half of the shops are shuttered, there's some foot traffic along the Miyakawa shopping street, and a few cyclists whizzing through with bikes full of groceries and small children. Recently, some signs of entrepreneurship are beginning to stir, including a small shop called Okomeya, which literally means "rice store."

The business was conceptualized by Atsuo Otsuka, who runs Owan, a small branding and design firm in the neighborhood. Saddened by his local neighborhood's decline, he started Okomeya with an eye to revitalizing the area. "My grandparents lived in Togoshi, but after they passed, their house was vacant. That's where my office—and Okomeya—began."

Otsuka is interested in selling not only rice, but rice-based products too. "The rice sold at Okomeya is the Koshihikari variety from Uonuma in Niigata Prefecture, grown by my relatives," says Otsuka. "There, farmers are exploring new applications for rice. Things like makeup, accessories, iPhone cases and brown rice coffee."

Atsushi Kabasawa, who sells fermented rice products out of the shop, heralds Otsuka's efforts to make Togoshi a little livelier. "Togoshi was a shuttered town, so how do we open the shutters?" he says. "That was the thought process at the beginning."

4-8-6 Togoshi
Shinagawa-ku
Tokyo 142-0041

Essay:
One Up, One Down

In Tokyo, many new houses are built with a sell-by date of roughly two decades. *Tim Hornyak* explores this scrap-and-build culture, and the role it has played in creating some of the city's most architecturally daring designs.

Left Photograph: © Tomio Ohashi; Right Photograph: © Akio Kawasumi

The Nakagin Capsule Tower (pictured) is a historic example of Tokyo's innovative approach to designing for small spaces.

In Italo Calvino's *Invisible Cities*, Marco Polo tells an aging Kublai Khan about the many fantastic places he claims to have visited. One is the metropolis of Thekla, a massive collection of "cranes pulling up other cranes, scaffoldings that embrace other scaffoldings, beams that prop up other beams." When asked why Thekla's construction is taking so long, the inhabitants respond, "So that its destruction cannot begin."

Polo might well have been describing the capital of Japan, which Calvino visited in 1976, instead of an imaginary city. Tokyo is a city of a thousand building sites, a vast patchwork of plots on which structures are built, used for a few decades, and then razed. It's an endless cycle of construction and destruction fueled by social mores, regulations and taxes, although a small but growing segment of Japanese architects are trying to challenge the existing framework.

On a macro level, Tokyo isn't a beautiful city. It encompasses a riot of architectural styles in full embrace of kitsch. A postwar wooden yakitori joint might be shoehorned between a newly poured *manshon* of exposed concrete and a megawatt pachinko parlor of mirror chrome. Add to this lexicon vast forests of neon, fluorescent and LED signs, overlay a spaghetti canopy of power lines, crisscross it all with railways, ring roads and cramped lanes, and you get an idea of the city's built environment. And don't forget the people: 13.7 million of them, living in the heart of a greater metropolitan area of 38 million.

This entity defies easy decoding. Tokyo is a mash of nearly 50 cities where most streets are nameless and addresses are nonsequential.

Above all, its sheer scale bewilders. Zoom out and each neon light is a dot in one of the countless capillaries of a vast artificial organism that has metastasized out of Tokyo Bay into Chiba, Saitama and Kanagawa, and far to the south into the foothills of Mount Fuji. As the seat of power of the Tokugawa shogunate, it was home to Edo Castle, one of history's largest fortresses. In samurai times, Edo was known as the city of 800 villages, which were linked by moats, roads and other defenses. Tokugawa planners eschewed the Chinese-style grid of Kyoto in favor of an organic, concentric and fortified design that exploited the natural topography of hills and mud flats while reclaiming land from the bay. This blueprint survived the many fires that swept the city, Japan's late 19th-century modernization program that transformed Edo into Tokyo, and two catastrophic events of the 20th century: the 1923 Great Kanto Earthquake and the 1945 US firebombing.

"As a result of the rebuilding, the construction industry grew and led the economy," says Yoshiyuki Yamana, a professor of architecture at Tokyo University of Science. "In order to sustain this industry, national events such as the 1964 Tokyo Olympics were promoted and saw the repeated remodeling of Tokyo. There is therefore no continuity in buildings forming the city, and it is sometimes expressed as a city of memory loss."

It's perhaps on the level of individual structures that Tokyo is easiest to grasp. The first home I stayed in was a friend's flimsy *apaato* from the 1960s in a back alley in Nakano. It consisted of a cramped kitchen, dining area and a tatami room with an outsized TV and a Sega Dream-

In most countries, the value of a building appreciates over time. In Japan, plots of land change hands in the expectation that the house standing on it will be demolished.

cast. I slept on a futon a few feet from a gas heater, but the November chill still crept through gaps in the *fusuma*. After I smacked the lintel with my forehead several times, I developed an instinctive need to bow. Still, I was fond of the place, and enjoyed folding my body like an origami crane into the avocado-green fiberglass bathtub. Years later, after having lived in Shinjuku and Shibuya, I retraced my first steps in Japan down that back alley only to find that the building had been replaced with a prefab structure clad in ersatz brick.

"It is an ancient Japanese belief that a house is only a temporary abode," the metabolist architect Kisho Kurokawa wrote. "If it burns down, it can easily be rebuilt." Impermanence and change define architecture in Tokyo. Wooden houses and even reinforced concrete buildings rarely last more than 40 years; commercial buildings that old are viewed as ancient. One popular bar, a basement space in Kagurazaka where the DJ spun Steely Dan vinyl on the turntable, shut after the 2011 earthquake, its building demolished because of minor structural damage. In Nakameguro, a gorgeous old-world house with an ornate wooden gate

and meticulously trimmed garden was suddenly replaced with a low-rise block of condos. In a former geisha quarter on the Sumida River, a postwar *ryotei* restaurant, where Japanese politicians sealed deals over sake and shamisen in the '60s, was pulled down to make way for a tower manshon. This is shrugged off as *shoganai*; unavoidable. But it can still be painful.

"There are several reasons for these short-term lifespans, but one big reason is that it is said that after 22 years, the property tax depreciation period for wooden houses expires and the real estate becomes worthless," says Yamana. "Other factors include keeping up with earthquake resistance standards and selling property to pay inheritance taxes. The increase of houses built on small plots of land is accelerating, as is the customization of wooden homes."

There is an upside to the churn. Though many single-family homes are unremarkable prefab units from the likes of Panasonic, Daiwa and Sekisui, architects are boldly experimenting with custom dwellings. The wanderer of Tokyo's great labyrinth can discover whimsical structures not only of wood but of concrete, steel and aluminum.

One example of small-lot creativity is House Tokyo by Junichi Sampei and ALX Architect, constructed on a 480-square-foot plot in 2010. Clad in white perforated steel, the building looks like a multifaceted alabaster obelisk without obvious openings; at night, the windows are apparent and it takes on the appearance of a traditional Japanese lamp. Inside, skylights admit light into a geometric collage of white and gray surfaces, exposed concrete, metallic stairways and a glass bridge. Go Hasegawa & Associates' Townhouse in Asakusa, completed in 2010, brings a surprising modernism to one of Tokyo's traditional districts, just like the Tokyo Skytree looming overhead. The four-story family residence has offset windows and skylights over a stack of mezzanines, which also serve as sleeping areas, around an open interior space that's topped with a sheltered rooftop terrace. "Due to the holes and the windows in the exterior walls and by altering the position of the skylights, you can look down diagonally at the neighborhood from the upper floors and look up at the windows from the lower floors," Hasegawa tells Philip Jodidio in his book *The Japanese House Reinvented*.

Hiroshi Matsukuma, a professor of architecture at Kyoto Institute of Technology and activist for preserving older architecture, is encouraged by projects in Tokyo neighborhoods such as Asakusa and Yanaka. "Japan, which reached its peak population and has entered an era of rapid demographic decline, should face the problem of destruction of architectural culture," says Matsukuma. "I am hoping that a change in consciousness that cherishes smaller places will progress amid urban development projects such as the 2020 Tokyo Olympics, the 2025 Osaka Expo and the construction of large-scale casinos. We need policies to establish a living environment where everyone can depend on one another, with our limited resources and population."

Large-scale events like the Olympics will leave their own legacy, but Tokyoites are increasingly keen on making, and perhaps preserving, their own spaces.

"It's on the level of individual structures that Tokyo is easiest to grasp."

4

Directory

STEPHANIE D'ARC TAYLOR

Cult Rooms

For Osaka's extravagant 1970 Expo, Isamu Noguchi created a propulsive and aqueous centerpiece.

After World War II, there came a point when Japan—exhausted by decades of nationalism and long-cloistered by its leaders for fear of cultural dilution—felt a powerful hunger for outside ideas. The artist and landscape architect Isamu Noguchi, the son of a Japanese father and white American mother, was uniquely positioned to introduce ideas that were familiar enough to be accessible, but exotic enough to feel progressive. Growing up in Japan, he was considered American; once he moved back to the United States to attend boarding school and then university, he was seen as Japanese (despite taking a white American name—Sam Gilmour—for a time). These symmetrical experiences of being "othered" in two places he could call home no doubt contributed to a clear sense of empathy, and activism, in his life's work.

For the 1970 Osaka Expo, Kenzo Tange, the founder of the metabolist movement, commissioned Noguchi to design a series of fountains. Never faint of heart, Noguchi used the commission as an opportunity to debut, on a heroic scale, ideas about how sculpture can spark community. In his work, designed in accordance with the theme *Dream for Space*, sculptures appear to be erupting from a huge rectangular pool, propelled skyward by streams of water. "Twelve enormous sculptures—cubes, spheres, and cylinders—bristling with jet nozzles, provided an exuberantly choreographed water display, dramatically illuminated at night," wrote Martin Friedman, the longtime director of the Walker Art Center in Minneapolis. One piece, a cube called *The Comet*, soars 100 feet into the air; two more, called *Spaceships*, are animatronic semispheres, bobbing up and down while shooting water in every direction. It was a dazzling centerpiece for the Expo, which was the biggest and most expensive world's fair ever, costing today's equivalent of $19 billion.

Water—carefully juxtaposed with stone according to Buddhist geomancy—is a traditional feature of Japanese gardens. In Western gardens and public art, fountains consist of a pool or sculpture from which water erupts in a pattern. With his propulsive design, Noguchi created something that belongs to both traditions, as well as one that is all his own.

A believer in the potential for art to improve society, Noguchi found an outlet for his decidedly populist work in 1930s Mexico. He collaborated with Diego Rivera on a large-scale mural for the Abelardo L. Rodriguez Market in Mexico City (and was taken as a lover by Rivera's wife, Frida Kahlo). During World War II, he volunteered to be interred at the Poston War Relocation Center—one of the American concentration camps where Japanese nationals living in the US were forced to relocate. An official resident of New York, Noguchi was exempt from detention. Still, he went to Poston as an expression of solidarity, and with the government-approved task of beautifying the camp.

Throughout his career, Noguchi proved himself to be an artist who cared little for disciplinary boundaries. Perhaps that was what drew the admiration of the young Tange, who frequently invited the older Noguchi to contribute to the grandiose architectural plans he and his acolytes in the metabolist movement became famous for. After collaborating on several such projects, including the Hiroshima Peace Park, Tange again looked to Noguchi when he won the contract to design the 1970 Osaka Expo.

Noguchi's fountains were turned off at the end of the Expo, in September 1970, and have remained dormant ever since. Last year, the Osaka prefectural government announced that six would be renovated, and switched on once more as part of a cultural conservation effort. Noguchi died in 1988, 30 years too early to see his floating fountains flowing again. Before his death, he was awarded both America's National Medal of Arts and the Order of the Sacred Treasure from Japan's government. The awards signaled appreciation and acceptance; perhaps Noguchi, at last, felt a sense of being at home in both worlds.

The Toast CEO on slowness as a solution.

BELLA GLADMAN

Suzie de Rohan Willner

Toast first launched in 1997 as a mail-order nightwear and loungewear company operating out of a barn in Wales. Its accompanying vision of a simpler yet richer life struck such a chord that, over two decades later, it's grown into a global business. Toast's palette of natural textures, organic colors and fluid lines (applied to a product list that has expanded into women's clothing and homeware) have won the sort of committed fans who treasure archive pieces as much as the latest collection. This year, Toast is launching New Makers—a long-term initiative through which the team will deploy their creative expertise in support of emerging designers. Here, *Suzie de Rohan Willner*, who joined as CEO in 2015, explains the importance of nurturing talent and extending Toast's "slow" ethos to office life.

BG: *Toast makes everything from bed linen to knitwear. What's the common thread?* **SRW:** When we talk to our customers, the first thing they say is that when they experience Toast, they slow down, whether they're standing in store, wearing our clothes or holding a hand-thrown mug. Our colors, the textures and the photography all convey a different pace—something that's apart from the speed of everyday life.

BG: *Do you carry that philosophy into the office?* **SRW:** Yes. It's present in everything we do. I think people would be surprised about how much we labor over each decision—the trim on a cuff, the smocking on a shoulder, the shape of a hem. We also take time to get to know everyone we work with, from our knitters and weavers to our ceramicists, writers and artists. Once a month in our London office, everyone comes together to sit at the big wooden dining table and listen to inspiring speakers.

BG: *What does slowness look like for a very busy person?* **SRW:** My daughter recently said, "You have no divide between work and life, Mum!" She's right—I'm passionate about what I do—but I carve out time for myself. I go on a retreat once a year. When I get up, I'll meditate, I'll do yoga. But it's about how you roll through the day. I use the beautiful things around me—colorful furniture, Toast pieces hanging on my office wall—as cues to pause.

BG: *Given Toast's simple aesthetic, how do you ensure you're not repeating yourself?* **SRW:** We have silhouettes that we love and which have stood the test of time, but each collection will always contain exciting new pieces and variations, and have different nods to certain periods or styles—whether it's Black Mountain College, Ingrid Bergman or Georgia O'Keeffe. We started our New Makers initiative so we could champion new designers. We wanted to share our expertise, and give them a platform to share their craft. They will receive full profit, but we benefit too—simply through learning about their craft and witnessing their passion for working with their hands.

BG: *How do you feel about slow fashion being so popular at the moment?* **SRW:** It's such a good thing, isn't it? Toast doesn't need to shout about having done it for a long time—we'll just continue along the path that we've always taken. We like to offer up thoughts, rather than dictate them. Personally, Toast has taught me to delight in clothes with longevity. As a young woman in Paris, I was a fashion victim; I used to spend every penny on clothes. I don't do that anymore! In our shops we run *Sashiko* repair workshops, teaching our customers the ancient Japanese technique of patching and repairing. This way they are able to give old garments a new life.

BG: *Do you have a favorite piece from Toast that you wear again and again?* **SRW:** The Kantha Quilted Coat. It started originally as a bed jacket, but people decided to wear it as outerwear—my mother wears it as a coat, and we've renamed it as such! Because they're made from recycled saris, you don't know exactly what you're going to get.

Each time I put it on I notice another small detail, something that makes me stop and wonder and appreciate the great skill, that's gone into it. It's pieces like this that bring joy, and slow us down.
—
This feature was produced in partnership with Toast.

For Rohan Willner, the right outfit can affect her outlook: She wears the Kantha Quilted Coat when giving career talks, as she feels it carries a quiet gravitas.

ELLIE VIOLET BRAMLEY

Power Showers

Why good ideas flow under water.

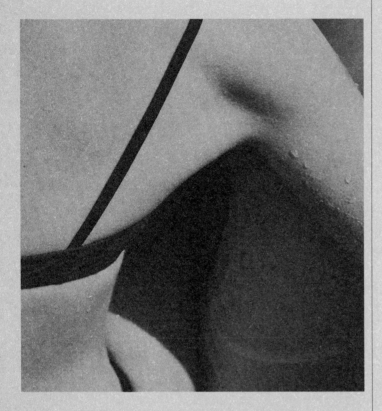

Whether you've just woken up or are about to go to bed, are sweaty from a run or need to warm up after a cold walk home, showers are a rejuvenating joy. They can also be a great place to think. According to a 2016 study by cognitive scientist Scott Barry Kaufman, 72 percent of people have their best ideas in the shower. If Reddit is anything to go by, they have weird ideas as well as good ones. The online forum's "showerthoughts" community is home to 16.3 million people sharing their "miniature epiphanies." Posts on the thread range from the existential: "You have existed since the beginning of the universe, but only realized it when you gained consciousness," to the very silly: "The trees cut down to make Jenga blocks are repeatedly forced to relive their own death." Or, as Snoop Dogg once informed his Twitter followers: "I just sat in the shower for an hour thinking about how Mercedes has 3 E's all pronounced differently."

Why is the shower such a good place for innovative, meaningful or just downright absurd thoughts? Could it be the meditative flow of water? Or perhaps the upright stance inspires an active mind (unlike a bath, where your hori-zontal position encourages sloth-fulness in mind and body). Perhaps it is both. And since certain aromas are thought to promote memory and alertness, using a shampoo that smells of rosemary, say, can't hurt either. Kaufman, speaking at a summit on "peak work performance" has another explanation: "The relaxing, solitary and non-judgmental shower environment may afford creative thinking by allowing the mind to wander freely," opening people up to their inner consciousness. Other scientists have credited dopamine—the "happy hormone." Often present when we have our best ideas, it can apparently be triggered by warm showers.

A shower is a total shift of pace and tone from whatever has gone before and, even if you have to make it snappy, you can usually switch to autopilot so that you're not thinking about the act of washing while doing it. It's one time of the day when checking your phone is challenging, as are other distractions like TV, radio and conversation. Short or long, your shower is an opportunity for your mind to meander. Got some thinking to do? Perhaps it's time to turn on the taps.

SOAP ON THE ROPES
by Harriet Fitch Little

The soap industry is all in a lather: Between 2010 and 2015, sales of bar soap declined by 5 percent in the US. The shift is partly due to the explosion of high-end, aggressively marketed liquid soap alternatives. (Remember, it was only a decade ago that the advertising industry realized that it could market shower gel to men as well as women.) It seems the use of bar soap is also falling, ironically, due to our obsession with being clean: Soap bars are now considered unhygienic, despite there being little evidence that bacteria on their surface can transfer from one wash to the next. Perhaps salvation will come in the form of our growing environmental consciousness; unlike gel, solid soap requires no packaging. (Top: Nail Brush by D R Harris. Center: Superfin Mexican Tuberose Soap by Buly 1803. Bottom: Geranium Leaf Body Scrub by Aesop.)

The cool history of a hot commodity.

Photograph: Aaron Tilley, Set Design: Niklas Hansen, Ice Styling: Tara Garnell

KATIE CALAUTTI

Object Matters: Ice

Ice as a natural element has been a fixture on earth for about 2.4 billion years. Ice as a commodity is a more recent phenomenon.

For centuries, ice was a luxury reserved for rich estate owners and used for food preservation rather than refreshment. That all changed in 1805, when a young Frederic Tudor was enjoying ice cream and cold drinks at his well-to-do Boston family's summer party and began musing about how colonizing forces in the West Indies would envy his refreshments.

Tudor became fixated on the idea of making ice into a commodity. His initial scheme was brilliant in theory, but it proved disastrous in execution: He decided to transport ice from the pond of his family's country estate to a place where people had never seen it—the Caribbean. Packed in straw for insulation, 130 tons of ice made the journey to Martinique in February of 1806—only to promptly melt when there proved no adequate storage facility.

But Tudor pressed on. He prevented meltage by tightly packing his ice with sawdust and working with locals to build ice houses near his ports. He also went on the road, practicing the infamous "first one is free" sales technique: offering guests chilled beverages at dinners, convincing bartenders that consumers preferred cold drinks and giving ice cream-making lessons to chefs.

Eventually, Tudor achieved the sort of paradigm shift that all entrepreneurs aspire to: He single-handedly transformed ice from a slippery byproduct of winter to a lucrative year-round necessity. He brought on foreman Nathaniel Wyeth, who revolutionized treacherous ice harvesting with horse-drawn grid plowing and tripled their production. A network of ice houses cropped up in the southern United States. Soon, Americans in cities couldn't live without ice during the sweltering summer.

By the 1840s, ice was being shipped all over the world and others were mimicking Tudor's methods. His enterprising idea ushered in the advent of refrigerators, freezers and at-the-ready cubes. It turns out that his methods proved prescient: Market something as indispensable, package it, and people will pay. Bottled water, anyone?

Artist and co-founder of London's Kinetica Museum *Dianne Harris* on the madcap genius of Swiss artist *Jean Tinguely*.

DIANNE HARRIS

Peer Review

It was really Jean Tinguely who invented and introduced the idea of performative art. From the 1950s onwards, he created sculptural machines that moved independently and made their own artworks and, in doing so, he recreated the role of the artist. One sculpture, *Homage to New York*, was built to destroy itself. He also made many *Métamatic* sculptures, which were autonomous art robots: They used a mechanical arm to make abstract drawings. The intrigue and uncertainty of what these machines would produce was pivotal to the development of art of future generations and paved the way for artists to work with new technologies.

I co-founded Kinetica Museum with Tony Langford in 2006. Since leaving art school in the early '90s I had been working within the film industry; I worked on *Frankenstein, Hackers, Judge Dredd*, and then went to live in San Francisco, enmeshed in the backlash of Silicon Valley and the robot revolution of the 1990s. I was interested in how man and machine could become one; the idea of merging realities has always been a huge subject for me.

Over the past 12 years, Kinetica has become a leading international platform showcasing innovative and multidisciplinary artists experimenting with new media. We also focus on exhibiting the historical lineage of kinetic art and its pioneers. Tinguely is a massive influence on anyone working with kinetic art today. In one of our shows, the artist Tim Lewis exhibited an autonomous robot that signs Dalí's signature over and over again; it was a work made using scrap metal, carved wood and archaic machinery, and it ended up in a show at the Tinguely Museum in Basel. Another pair of artists, Ben Parry and Jacques Chauchat, made a kinetic *Sonic Junk Machine*—a milk truck covered in animatronic discarded objects of everyday life which became an orchestra of discord. They drove that through London—their homage to Tinguely.

The past 15 years have seen a massive resurgence in kinetic art. Kinetica has been a huge part of that, exhibiting artists who are using new materials and technology and warping and twisting them to create new ideas. Artists are always at the forefront of innovation and invention as they are free to experiment without any boundaries. Tinguely created a machine which turned on itself. That's a revolutionary idea!

Photograph: Robert Doisneau/Gamma-Rapho/Getty Images

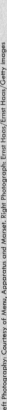
Left Photography: Courtesy of Menu, Apparatus and Marset. Right Photograph: Ernst Haas/Ernst Haas/Getty Images

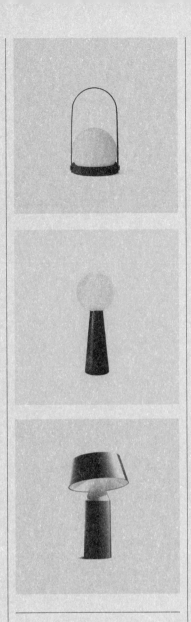

ETERNAL FLAME
by Harriet Fitch Little

For at least a century, wounded lovers have healed their breakups with sad ballads known as "torch songs." As Adele croons on "Someone Like You": "I had hoped you'd see my face / And that you be reminded that for me it isn't over." The phrase "torch song" derives from the idea of "carrying a torch" for someone—a saying that gained currency in the 1920s. Some have tried to link its origins to the ancient Greek tradition of lighting torches to celebrate wedding nuptials. More likely, it's just a poetic way of picturing a broken heart: If love is a fire that makes two people glow as one, then what better way to describe the sad, lonely light that only one person carries forward than as a torch? (Top: Carrie LED Lamp by Menu. Center: Neo Lantern by Apparatus. Bottom: Bicoca Portable Lamp by Marset.)

CHARLES SHAFAIEH

Drill Down

Is the future of urban living underground?

By 2050, the United Nations predicts that over two-thirds of the world's population will live in urban areas. To many architects, the most appealing response to this influx is to build vertically. But rather than continuing to colonize the sky by erecting skyscrapers which, as they grow taller, embody ever-louder expressions of bravado, why not consider constructing in the opposite direction?

The idea of going underground is gaining favor. In Mexico City, for example, architecture firm BNKR Arquitectura has proposed a 65-story inverted pyramid—the "Earthscraper"; this nod to the city's Aztec history could house 5,000 people underneath the Plaza de la Constitución. Singapore and other Asian metropolises have also begun subterranean exploration in response to population booms. Doing so pushes against popular conceptions of the underground as a burial zone or a space occupied by the living only while in transit or as a short-term refuge from extreme weather and war.

Such innovation does, however, retain the transgressive identity of "the underground." The privacy afforded by being belowground has long prompted clandestine behavior, such as the habits of the 18th-century Hellfire Club—a group of high-society men, including the painter William Hog-arth—whose debauchery echoed throughout a system of caves excavated into the English countryside. In the 21st century, isolation has a radical appeal beyond licentiousness: Underground spaces could become sites that encourage privacy and solitude, as opposed to the panoptic skyscrapers that put their inhabitants on display in an already over-surveilled world.

Through their lack of windows and often mazelike, arterial configurations, subterranean spaces confuse our sense of time and space. These characteristics prime them for journeys, both literal and metaphorical. No wonder, then, that they attract architects designing art institutions such as Helsinki's Amos Rex Museum, whose 14,000 square feet lie below Lasipalatsi Square. Inherently strange and disorienting, these spaces heighten ambiguities and nurture enigmatic experiences. Ancient cultures grasped this potential, too, as evinced by the recurring trope in myths of the living—including Homer's Ulysses and Virgil's Aeneas—traveling to the underworld. Called *katabasis* in ancient Greek, these journeys can foster deep introspection and transformation. Rather than focusing on what we can see, like a plant's flowers, the idea of going underground encourages us to consider our strong, buried roots.

Complete the starred clues to redefine Tokyo.

ANNA GUNDLACH

Crossword

ACROSS

1. He flew too close to the sun
7. Where cattle are collected
14. Put the ___ on (stop)
15. Like a lot of press conference answers
16. Tokyo, translated literally, and what the answers to the starred clues literally have & spell
18. It's sipped in French restaurants
19. Kate McKinnon's show
20. *Completes a task precisely as asked
28. Did as told
29. Like some sci-fi body parts
33. Lifter put under a dorm bed's leg
34. *1954 French erotic novel by Pauline Réage
36. Class for U.S. immigrants
37. It smells, but doesn't stink
38. Relative of .gov
39. *Kellogg's cereal and snack bar brand
42. J.K. Rowling's Malfoy
44. Japanese automotive giant
45. Benghazi resident
46. *Millennials, by another name
49. Australian source of meat & oil
52. Caboose
53. *Red, fruity, jiggly dessert
62. Warrior in a classic Akira Kurosawa film
63. Put down
64. Exude
65. "Same here!"

DOWN

1. Mike's candy partner
2. Source of some WikiLeaks docs
3. Planking works them
4. Turn, like food in a compost bin
5. Reason for existing
6. Extremely savvy
7. Do some new editing on an old film
8. "Selma" director DuVernay
9. Conk out for a few
10. TV series with Miami and Cyber spinoffs
11. Billboard Hot 100 listings
12. Tony-winner Dear ___ Hansen
13. List on Depop
17. "It Was Written" rapper
20. Setting for many fairy tales
21. San Luis ___, CA
22. Stahl of "60 Minutes"
23. Caustic chemical used in making soap and bagels
24. Contraction in "The Star Spangled Banner" and "Jingle Bells"
25. Wind instrument with a distinct tone
26. It's only about 20% oxygen
27. Fidget spinner or Tamagotchi
30. Request to someone making your sandwich, maybe
31. "...assuming it's possible for me"
32. Group in an ant farm
34. Fa-la link
35. "For shame"
37. Bread with tikka masala
40. Small part of a big machine
41. Suffix that means "resident"
42. Morse code bit
43. Stat for Ichiro
45. Prince Harry's mom, familiarly
47. Spine-chilling
48. GI's time off
49. Gaelic language
50. Southern term of address
51. West Point school, for short
54. "A horse has a stable personality," e.g.
55. Clothing with hooks
56. Have some sashimi, say
57. Martin Sheen's "West Wing" role
58. Angsty and sensitive, slangily
59. Allow
60. Southeast Asian ethnic group
61. Tokyo-born "Double Fantasy" singer

THE LAST WORD

Every day, some 40 million commuters brave the Tokyo rail network—a highly sophisticated but perennially overcrowded rapid transit system. *Selena Hoy*, who spent weeks whizzing around the city to compile this issue's Tokyo City Guide, shares her tips for surviving *tsukin jigoku*—"commuter hell."

Tokyo's train system is a sprawling beast with many tendrils. Every day, it transports millions of people from one corner of the metropolis to another along its vast network. Part of what makes it all run so smoothly is that everyone knows where they're going, and how to get there. Personal space is limited and stress runs high during commuting times, so the goal is to melt into the river of people without disrupting the flow.

There are ways to make movement more manageable. Everyone lines up neatly for the train, waiting for passengers to disembark before boarding. If you break these rules, it's unlikely that anyone will reprimand you,

but there may be an aggrieved glance or a sharp elbow nudge for upsetting the social order. Those who want to avoid becoming intimately acquainted with a stranger's pores while having their own organs rearranged on a sardine-packed train can steer clear of morning and evening rush hours (around 7:30-9 a.m. and 5:30-7 p.m.). And women worried about groping can use women-only cars at the ends of many trains during morning rush hour.

Not feeling the allure? Much of central Tokyo is walkable and bikeable. The best thing about the city is the endless discovery, the constant change, upheaval, and renewal. Learn to get lost.

MUUTO

Stockists

AESOP
aesop.com

AMBUSH
ambushdesign.com

APPARATUS
apparatusstudio.com

BUILDING BLOCK
building--block.com

BULY 1803
buly1803.com

CECILIE BAHNSEN
ceciliebahnsen.com

CELINE
celine.com

COMMON PROJECTS
commonprojects.com

D. R. HARRIS
drharris.co.uk

DIOR
dior.com

DIPTYQUE
diptyqueparis.com

DOMESTIQUE PARIS
domestiqueparis.com

DYSON
dyson.com

ERES
eresparis.com

EVERYDAY NEEDS
everyday-needs.com

HANDVAERK
handvaerk.com

HERMÈS
hermes.com

HOUSE OF FINN JUHL
finnjuhl.com

HYKE
hyke.jp

ISSEY MIYAKE
isseymiyake.com

IT'S YONOBI
itsyonobi.com

JENS
j-e-n-s.jp

JOHN LAWRENCE SULLIVAN
john-lawrence-sullivan.com

LAMBERT & FILS
lambertetfils.com

LAULHÈRE PARIS
laulhere-store.com

LAURENCE BOSSION
laurencebossion.com

LINDBERG
lindberg.com

LINUM
linumdesign.com

LOUIS VUITTON
louisvuitton.com

MAISON MARGIELA
maisonmargiela.com

MAISON MICHEL
michel-paris.com

MARC JACOBS
marcjacobs.com

MARSET
marset.com

MENU
menu.as

MISTER IT
misterit.jp

MORGAN LANE
morgan-lane.com

MR PORTER
mrporter.com

MUTINA
mutina.it

MUUTO
muuto.com

MYKITA
mykita.com

PAPIER LABO
papierlabo.com

PARACHUTE HOME
parachutehome.com

PETIT BATEAU
petit-bateau.com

RALPH LAUREN
ralphlauren.com

RETROSUPERFUTURE
retrosuperfuture.com

RIMOWA
rimowa.com

ROCHAS
rochas.com

SANDRO
sandro-paris.com

SPORTMAX
sportmax.com

STRING
string.se

STUDIO MUMBAI
studiomumbai.com

SUN BUDDIES
sunbuddieseyewear.com

SYURO
syuro.info

TAKEO
takeo.co.jp

TOAST
toa.st

TOTOKAELO ARCHIVE
totokaelo.com

YAECA HOME STORE
yaeca.com

YOHEI OHNO
yoheiohno.com

YOHJI YAMAMOTO
yohjiyamamoto.co.jp

YUKI HASHIMOTO
yuki-hashimoto.com

LINUM

ISSUE 32

Credits

COVER
Photographer
Romain Laprade
Stylist
Daisuke Hara
Hair & Makeup
Shimonagata Ryoki
Model
Hiromi Yamamura
Photography Assistant
Antoine Laffitte
Art Director & Producer
Kevin Pfaff
Production Assistant
Shoko Nakanishi

Hiromi wears a coat by Hermès.

P. 64 – 79
Hair
Taan Doan
Makeup
Cyril Laine
Casting
Sarah Bunter
Model
Stephanie Omorojor at Elite London
Model
Julien Pernot at Elite Paris
Styling Assistant
Candy Hagedorn

P. 64
Julien wears a shirt by Ralph Lauren, shorts by Hermès and uses Hermès binoculars.

P. 124 - 135
Model
Hiromi Yamamura at Fridayfarm
Model
Keisuke at CDU Models
Hair & Makeup
Shimonagata Ryoki
Photography Assistant
Antoine Laffitte
Art Director & Producer
Kevin Pfaff
Production Assistant
Shoko Nakanishi

P. 124
Hiromi wears a dress by Hyke and a slip dress by Mister It. *Keisuke* wears a jacket by Yuki Hashimoto, a shirt by Issey Miyake Men and trousers by Jens.

P. 142 - 149
Retouching
Karin Eriksson

P. 154 - 171
Production Assistants
Shoko Nakanishi
Yurina Okamoto
Photography Assistant
Antoine Laffitte

Special Thanks:
Mako Ayabe
Kota Engaku
Nikolaj Hansson
Noriko Kobayashi at LOG
Kaori Miyazaki at Gi-Co-Ma
Yurina Okamoto
Kevin Pfaff
Susan Rogers Chikuba
Antoine & Joëlle Viaud
Nanako Yamaguchi